Long After

MIDNIGHT

at the Niño Bien

BRIAN
WINTER

Long After

MIDNIGHT

at the Niño Bien

A YANQUI'S MISSTEPS IN ARGENTINA

WILLIAM HEINEMANN: LONDON

Published by William Heinemann, 2008

2 4 6 8 10 9 7 5 3 1

Copyright © Brian Winter, 2007

Brian Winter has asserted his right under the Copyright, Designs
and Patents Act 1988 to be identified as the author of this work

First published in the United States in 2008 by Public Affairs™,
a member of the Perseus Books Group

First published in Great Britain in 2008 by
William Heinemann
Random House, 20 Vauxhall Bridge Road,
London SW1V 2SA

www.rbooks.co.uk

Addresses for companies within The Random House Group Limited
can be found at: www.randomhouse.co.uk/offices.htm

The Random House Group Limited Reg. No. 954009

A CIP catalogue record for this book
is available from the British Library

ISBN: 9780434016112

The Random House Group Limited supports The Forest Stewardship
Council (FSC), the leading international forest certification
organisation. All our titles that are printed on Greenpeace approved
FSC certified paper carry the FSC logo. Our paper procurement policy
can be found at: www.rbooks.co.uk/environment

Mixed Sources
Product group from well-managed
forests and other controlled sources
www.fsc.org Cert no. TT-COC-2139
FSC © 1996 Forest Stewardship Council

Book Design by Jeff Williams

Printed and bound in Great Britain by
CPI Mackays, Chatham, ME5 8TD

For Erica

Fall in love, fall in love. That's my only advice.
It can be with a girl, or with the music, or with the
dance. It doesn't matter. But, whatever you do, fall
in love. And, if you do this, then the tango, with all
the bullshit that you'll go through along the way,
will have been worth it for you.

— "THE GODFATHER"

A popular Argentine joke goes:

Q. How does an Argentine commit suicide?
A. By jumping off his own ego.

Thus, to protect the inflated (but very, very fragile) self-esteem of friends and acquaintances in the world of the *milonga*, where reputation is everything, I have changed some of the characters' names and identifying characteristics in this book. The chronology of some events has also been modified for storytelling purposes.

Long After

MIDNIGHT

at the Niño Bien

part one

REVOLUTIONS
AND TANGOS

A FEW MONTHS BEFORE THE SUPERMARKET RIOTS STARTED, I had asked El Tigre to give me my first tango lesson. He looked me up and down, his eyebrows wrinkled with disdain, his eyes halting on my mud-stained tennis shoes. "I don't traffic in miracles," he sighed, knocking back the rest of his double-malt whisky, the color slowly returning to his weathered face. "And that's obviously what's needed here, so you'd better start praying to whichever god you prefer. I make no promises. But, if you meet me next Thursday at midnight outside the door at the Niño Bien, I'll give you my best effort."

The following week, I dutifully did as told, and I even managed to borrow a freshly buffed pair of black dress shoes for the occasion. At a quarter till one, El Tigre finally materialized out of the shadows and into the copper glow of the streetlight, his colossal frame practically floating down the sidewalk. He had a grin on his face, and his fingers were twitching with nervous anticipation. "To war," he whispered with a nod. We bounded up the marble stairway of the old Leonese cultural center two steps at a time, paid our five-peso admission, and turned the corner into the Niño Bien's grand salon.

Inside, the girls were swarming like honeybees. El Tigre was already just a bit too drunk to swat them away as we fought through the crowd, struggling to make our way to our table. Waitresses with gold teeth, the bar girl in her wine-speckled blouse, the dancers in their delicate fishnet stockings—they savagely elbowed each other out of the way, kissing him hello on the cheek, hanging from his knotted arms, giggling at his every compliment. It took us half an hour just to sit down.

Nobody there knew his real name; at tango halls around the city, El Tigre was known solely by his nom de guerre. He claimed to know nothing of its origin. "I was just walking down the street one day and this girl from the *milonga* saw me and said, 'Hey, Tiger!' That's the truth. She said the other girls called me that." He shrugged, flashed a devious grin, and added, in a rumbling, theatrical growl: "I can't imagine why."

"Do you get a lot of girls?" I asked him as we settled into our chairs.

"That's not important. I come to dance the tango. If I go home with a beautiful woman, then that's fine. But it's not why I go out."

"But do you get a lot of girls?"

"Oh yes," he said quietly, solemnly. "El Tigre has had many women. But I'll tell you a secret," he said, leaning in and whispering into my ear: "If it weren't for the tango, I wouldn't have gotten laid since 1985."

El Tigre was about sixty years old—"No true *milonguero* ever reveals his exact age," he admonished me—and he had variously led the lives of a professional tango dancer, a budding film star, and a self-proclaimed man of the world. His black trousers sagged under a slight paunch, and a halfway-unbuttoned maroon silk shirt draped over his chest like old stage curtains. He wasn't outwardly handsome, and he was missing some of his front teeth, but when El Tigre smiled, a web of well-defined, friendly lines fanned out across his face, making him look a bit like a good-natured comic-book gangster. He claimed (somewhat dubiously) to be of mixed Italian and Spanish descent, and his accent was markedly lower class, the product of a childhood spent in Dock Sud, the rough-and-tumble port area of Buenos Aires.

"It was the Bronx of Argentina," he declared grandly. "It was where all the new immigrants came off the boats and lived first. We had blacks from Cape Verde, Italians, Spaniards, Chinese, Polish. . . . There were even a couple of English sailors who came through there. When we were kids, we'd run up to them and yell the only English we knew: '*Delta Line! Blue Star Line! Royal Bank! Good morning!*' Most of it we learned from reading the crates on the ships that came in."

"Was it a good place to grow up?"

"Sure it was!" El Tigre boasted, smiling. "Argentina offered all sorts of possibilities back then. Lots of people went on to get rich and do great things. Sort of like the Bronx, right? Al Pacino and Robert De Niro are from the Bronx, aren't they?"

I told him I wasn't sure.

"Well, if they had been from Argentina, De Niro and Pacino definitely would have been from Dock Sud," El Tigre concluded with a proud nod.

All conversation halted as a young woman of about twenty rose confidently from her table on the other side of the room and, improbably, began strutting toward us. Her curly, Goldilocks-blonde hair was yanked back violently into a bun, and her body was graced by a black strapless dress that seemed to cover progressively less of her body as she drew closer. I spotted her the second she got up—and so did everyone else in the room, as if they had been secretly spying on her all along. The men stared shamelessly, and the women jealously glared out of the corners of their eyes, picking apart her every move. In a country where people love nothing more than to stare and (better yet) be stared at, she confidently crossed the length of the room and, yes, oh my God, she really *was* walking toward us. Her lips parted to unveil a teasing smile as she sat down unabashedly in El Tigre's lap.

"Hello, Tigre," she cooed, wagging her finger at him. "You never called me."

El Tigre let her twist in the wind for a moment before rewarding her with a tight-lipped, self-conscious smile, subtly concealing his missing teeth. "Hello, dear," he rumbled in a much deeper voice than I had heard him use, one apparently reserved just for the ladies. "I'd like you to meet my new friend." He gestured toward me with a broad sweep of his giant hand.

She noticed me for the first time. I managed to hold her attention for exactly half a second. "Hello," she said politely, but her brown eyes had already focused back on the old stud as she shifted around in his lap, her hips burrowing deeper into his. Admired from close quarters, she looked much bonier, even malnourished. But she retained an alluring aura that suggested experience, and lots of it.

"It has been so dull around here," she sighed. "Did you go last week to The. . . . "

"Would you like to dance, dear?"

She beamed with euphoria—jackpot. "Of course!" she blurted, jumping to her feet and extending her slender hand.

"But I have to answer a few more questions from my friend first," El Tigre said, apologetic but firm, the consummate gentleman. "I'll come looking for you in a few moments, dear. I won't be long."

And, just like that, the beauty was dismissed. Her smile vanished, and her upper lip stiffened for a moment before she nodded, slowly turned, and walked away. At the surrounding tables, the whispers about her picked up in volume and cruelty as she crossed back to her spot in the dark, anonymous far corner of the room.

"That's really not necessary," I said, bewildered. "We can finish later. . . . "

"Nah, it's good for them to suffer a bit." He grinned, leaning back triumphantly in his chair. "That way, they don't expect anything."

"Oh . . . oh. Are you two. . . . "

"I'll never tell," El Tigre cut me off severely, frowning. "It's not gentlemanly."

"I'm sorry."

"Of course we're together!" he cackled, his lie of a frown gone, the lines on his face deepening mischievously. "Look at her! She's like a dog in heat! No commitment though," he said, pounding the table for emphasis and turning deadly serious for real this time. "No commitment. A tiger does not allow himself to be trapped under any circumstances."

We chuckled at that until Luis—the club's owner, who actually did bear an unsettling resemblance to Al Pacino, circa *Godfather II*—cautiously approached our table. "Can I get you gentlemen anything to drink?"

El Tigre frowned and turned to me, all business. "You're paying, right?"

His bluntness caught me off guard. I recovered quickly. "Sure. My pleasure."

"Johnny Walker black label with a splash of Coca Cola."

The blood drained out of Luis' face. "I'm sorry," he mumbled. "We're temporarily out. Problems with . . . the crisis. But I can offer you something else."

El Tigre gave Luis a dismissive wave of the hand and sighed in disgust. "Should we start my lesson now?" I asked.

"Rule number one," he boomed, his baritone brimming with verve. "Whisky, *then* tango. While we wait, though, I suppose you would like to hear how I came to dance a little tango with Madonna."

Eduardo Ayala—not yet baptized El Tigre—started learning tango on street corners when he was about thirteen. There were no formal classes back then, just a bunch of guys practicing—with each other, "obviously." The only women who casually danced the tango in Dock Sud back then were prostitutes. At one neighborhood social club, between jitterbugs to Elvis and the Beatles, the DJ would play intervals of tango, and only then was it possible to dance with a "decent" girl. It was there that Eduardo witnessed the man he considered the greatest milonguero of all time, a crippled old man with a metal screw in his hip. "When he walked he had this horrible limp, but when he danced, nothing," he recalled breathlessly. "I have never seen anything like him since. He was the master. We all watched for hours and hours, desperate to learn."

During the 1960s, the tango had entered a long era of decline, so there were only a few, very elite Argentines who could make a living by globe-trotting and dancing. Eduardo, who had dropped out of school after the sixth grade, answered the calling of a child from the port and put out to sea. He worked for three decades as an engine repairman for the merchant marine, steaming to ports of call all around the world, visiting every continent except the one closest to home: Antarctica. Faithful to his true passion, he did whatever he could to dance tango wherever possible.

"You would be shocked at some of the places where you could go tango. In Japan, for example, you would say those people have nothing in common with us Argentines. But they're tango fanatics! And very orderly and polite when they dance, I should add. I went to Iran once, and you can't dance there. But in Algeria, you can. Finland, that place is crazy about the tango. They have their own music and everything. Isn't the world marvelous?"

One night, somewhere out in that marvelous world, someone with an eye for talent asked Eduardo to teach him a few steps. The old sailor must have worked wonders because soon, in between dwindling assignments for the merchant marine, foreigners were buying him plane tickets to Paris and Rome so he could give classes there. This might have surprised a more humble man, but Eduardo, like all great Argentine tango dancers, knew quality when he saw it—in the mirror. "People watched me, they liked the way I danced, so they started asking me for lessons," he said casually, like it was the most natural thing in the world. "Teaching pleased me."

"Didn't that seem strange at first?" I pressed.

"Not really. I was very good. People liked my style."

"Who was the first person to ask you for a class?"

"I don't remember," he shrugged. "But that was when I started to become El Tigre."

Left to focus on his first and only true love, El Tigre—no longer Eduardo, mind you—lived the high life teaching repressed Americans, Germans, and Norwegians how to be Latin and visceral, if just for a day.

Some people simply lead charmed lives, while others are left to make their own good fortune. El Tigre liked to present himself as the former—for some reason, Argentines always believed it was better to be lucky than good—but it was clear that El Tigre had spent a good deal of effort, over the years, putting himself in the right place at the right time. Such was the case in 1994, when a purportedly random casting call for tango dancers in Buenos Aires turned out to be a search for extras for *Evita*, the movie adapted from the Broadway musical about Argentina's most famous first lady, Eva Perón. Madonna played the title role. One evening, the cast and crew went out for a night on the town in Buenos Aires, and everybody got a little boozed up. El Tigre claimed to have "accidentally" found himself tangoing with the Material Girl herself. "She was very nice, very simple," he said. "Her Spanish was quite good."

"Did she dance well?" I asked.

El Tigre gagged, choking on the ice at the bottom of his cheap, locally made whiskey. He stuttered several aborted replies before exploding into nervous, uncontrolled laughter. "Who cares? I danced with Madonna!" he bellowed. It was the only time I would ever see him uncomfortable. He chuckled, gazed into the bottom of his glass, and muttered to himself, "What else could you want?"

By this point we were both on drink number three and had long since given up making eye contact when we spoke, mutually content to focus instead on the never-ending hordes of gorgeous women flowing mercilessly into the dance hall. El Tigre heaved a deep sigh, his heavy shoulders finishing lower than before, as if a new burden had been placed upon them. "Madonna was very pretty," he said softly, "but I'll tell you this: she had nothing on these spectacular Argentine women."

"You're a man of the world," I said. "Is it true what they say about the Argentine girls?"

"Oh yes, certainly," he blurted, more sure of this than anything else he said that night. "The *argentinas* are the prettiest girls in the world. Of that there can be no doubt."

"Why do you think that is?" I asked. "Why are they so pretty?"

"Why? What kind of question is that?" El Tigre retorted, genuinely offended. "*Why?* No, no, no. This has always been a spectacular country. Argentina is superlative. Period. Don't ever forget that. Think about all the marvels this country has."

"There's the Pampa," I offered, hoping to redeem myself.

"And the splendor of Buenos Aires!"

"Lakes and deserts," I added. "Mountains and forests."

"Oil, silver, and gold!" El Tigre exclaimed, nearly shouting now. "Soy, corn, and wheat!"

"The widest avenue in the world!"

"The best *carne* in the world!" he cackled. "And I'm not talking about the cows!"

El Tigre pounded the table, making our empty glasses shake with each strike, quaking with laughter. Tears streamed down his cheeks. I craned my neck and motioned to Luis for another round. When I turned back to El Tigre barely a second had passed—but he had abruptly stopped laughing. His mood had gone from day to night. I followed his gaze and saw that he was fixated on the blonde waif in the black strapless dress, who had apparently given up waiting on El Tigre and was now out on the dance floor, blissfully tangoing in the arms of another man.

He shook his head in disgust. "It makes you think, doesn't it?"

"What?"

"How can a country with so much wealth, with so much beauty, end up like *this*?"

He downed what was left of his whiskey and stared hungrily at the girl, supporting his huge head with his hand. By now, it was well past 3 A.M., peak hour at the Niño Bien, and the cacophony of laughter, flirting, piano, and guitar was almost deafening. As the minutes ticked by, something about the music and noise seemed to thaw El Tigre's melancholy, and a tentative smile returned to his face. "What the hell," he sighed. "I think the time has come for your lesson to start."

"Okay," I said. "So what should I do?"

"Well, you go dance, *boludo*!"

I tried to stand up, but my head was spinning so badly that I collapsed back into my chair.

"But remember rule number two," El Tigre whispered, looking vaguely proud of me all of a sudden. "Only dance with the pretty ones. That's what the tango is for. Otherwise," he concluded, a smile illuminating his gangster's face, "you might as well just stay at home with your dick in your hand. And that's not why you're really here, is it?"

T HE NIGHT BEFORE I BOARDED THE PLANE SOUTH, A FAMILY friend exclaimed: "Oh, so you're moving to Argentina! Are you going to learn to tango?"

Well, no, I thought. I'm going to eat steak and have adventures and meet beautiful women and visit Patagonia, and then I'll go spectacularly broke and probably starve and limp back home and sell a kidney, and then I'll finally start my "real" grown-up life.

Sure, I had other, ever so slightly more profound, reasons for wanting to move to the end of the world—but tango certainly was not one of them. Back home, what little tango I'd seen seemed like more of a silly parody than an actual dance. It was performed only in Broadway shows and Hollywood movies, the sort of thing mere mortals would never in their wildest dreams think to try. The tango seemed to consist of: a man in something like a zoot suit, a woman in a sequined leotard, cheeks pressed together, roses clenched in teeth, lots of kicking and jumping, and clownishly pained expressions. It looked overwrought and stale and not like very much fun. For someone like me with zero natural dancing talent, the tango seemed utterly inaccessible, better left to the likes of Marlon Brando, Robert Duvall, and El Tigre's hero, Al Pacino.

Instead, I thought maybe I would find a job teaching English. Maybe I would work for an American corporation. Or maybe I would simply end up back home in six weeks, hat in hand. In truth, I hadn't really thought the whole thing through. There seemed no need to. I had come of age during a time when seemingly intelligent people were saying that war and the business cycle and perhaps history itself were things of the past. Whatever problems remained in the world, globalization would surely soon fix. Everybody I went to college with was receiving jaw-dropping job offers from dot-coms, and the only question that seemed to matter during our last semester was, "how big is your signing bonus?" At our graduation ceremony, the keynote speaker actually congratulated us for finishing our education rather than accepting a lucrative package with one of the local tech start-ups. It all seemed rather unreal, even then, but there was no tangible reason to think it would ever end.

My classmates spent those signing bonuses on plasma TVs and immediately began working sixty-hour weeks out of the airport Hilton in Chicago or Kansas City. This made some of them very happy. Yet, I had designs on becoming a journalist one day, and the most momentous news event so far in my very short adulthood had been a blow job in the Oval Office—not exactly the sort of thing that had forged Hemingway. I was seeking something simple but elusive—experience—and I felt, as if propelled by some kind of magnetic force, that I had to go as far away as possible to get it. I wanted to go someplace where the stars in the sky were different. Though I would have never phrased it this way at the time, I suppose I wanted to measure myself as a man by putting myself in an extraordinary situation, just for the hell of it.

Put another way: I had no idea what I was getting myself into.

I wanted to go somewhere that I could have an adventure, where things still *happened*. Latin America seemed like just that sort of place. Perhaps the days of midnight coups and banana republics had forever passed, but at least the history there was recent, like a fresh coat of paint. And who knew? Maybe I would get to see some kind of hiccup, a last gasp of a troubled, more dramatic era. As for Argentina, I knew it had great grass-fed steak; that Evita had been a whore; that fugitive Nazis had found it rather hospitable; that the water went down the toilet the wrong way; and that was about it. Argentina appealed to me primarily because of where it was on the map: at the very bottom. It seemed to be the anti-Texas. Meanwhile, I had spent a semester abroad in Spain (hadn't everybody?), so I believed the language wouldn't be a problem. So, two months after my college graduation, with an open-ended plane ticket in my hand, about $2,000 in savings in my bank account, no job, a free place to stay, and precisely two telephone numbers for friends of friends of friends who lived in Argentina, off I went.

On just my second day in Buenos Aires, I had been wandering, still strangely unaware of my new surroundings, through a street fair outside the Retiro train terminal when I heard a tinny radio playing. I was on a quest to buy an alarm clock, hoping in a rush of blind optimism that one day I might actually need one to wake me up so I could go somewhere important. Retiro was where newly arrived immigrants had once left the port city for a promising new life on the Pampa, but these days, most trains had stopped running; the operator had gone bankrupt, and Retiro was now mostly a place to buy either suspiciously cheap trinkets from China or even more suspiciously cheap *super pancho* hot dogs from God knows where. The terminal's ornate façade, which had once been a convincing replica of the station in Milan, was now covered with soot and graffiti. The street merchants let the clock alarms go off all day to show they weren't pirated fakes (you always had to be careful in Argentina), so that the whole market sounded like a nest of shrill, beeping baby birds. Amid the awful din, someone had thoughtfully turned on this old radio, and the unmistakable sound of tango crackled through the blown-out speakers.

The voice, incongruously happy and bright, sang:

> *The world was and always will be a piece of shit,*
> *This much I know.*
> *In the year 506, and in 2000 also!*
> *There have always been crooks, backstabbers, and suckers,*
> *But that the twentieth century is a spectacle of insolent evil,*
> *No one can deny.*

A bespectacled middle-aged woman behind one of the booths watched me pause to listen, and she noticed the expression on my face.

"You like that?" she called out to me in a smoky baritone. "That's our national anthem, you know."

"What's it called?"

"*Cambalache.*"

My Spanish was already passable in those days, but the word was new to me. "What does that mean?" I asked.

"Cambalache?" the woman repeated, caught off guard by the question. "I don't know . . . Cambalache means . . . cambalache." She put down her newspaper, took off her bifocals, and a wry grin crossed her face, as if she immensely enjoyed having something new to roll around in her head. "Hugo!" she yelled across the sidewalk. "Hugo, this young gentleman here wants to know what 'cambalache' means!"

Hugo was hunched on a wooden stool peddling yellowed literary magazines and Marxist propaganda. He looked like he had been in the exact same pose for the last thirty years. He regarded me severely for a moment before his face brightened. That day, just like every other day for the next four years, I couldn't avoid looking obviously, painfully foreign. But in Buenos Aires, uniquely among places I'd visited, being foreign almost always made people treat me *better*— even if they eventually found out I was from Texas.

"You're traveling?" Hugo enquired with a knowing smile. "Wandering about a bit, are you?"

"In reality," I said, "I just moved to Argentina. I'm living here."

His eyebrows raised. "*Why* would you do that?"

"I don't quite know."

"How strange," Hugo mused. "All of us are trying to get out of Argentina, and you come here! But that's fantastic. How lovely. Welcome."

"Thank you."

"You'll discover that Argentina is a marvelous country— too bad the people are such shit."

I could think of no adequate response to that, so I pretended to leaf through a copy of Juan Perón's book *Latin America: Now or Never* while I listened to the final verse of the strange song on Hugo's radio:

Twentieth century, cambalache
Problematic and feverish!
If you don't cry, you don't get to nurse,
And if you don't steal, you're a fool. . . .
Nobody cares if you were born honest.
It's all the same:
If you work day and night like an ox
If you live off others
If you kill, if you heal
Or if you live outside the law!

With two final, emphatic crashes of the piano, the radio went silent.

At that very moment, as those almost inconceivably cynical and bizarre lyrics echoed inside my head, I think it finally dawned on me for the first time that I was five thousand miles away from home in a strange country I knew next to nothing about.

This epiphany must have been telegraphed all over my face, because Hugo felt compelled to reach across the table and put a comforting hand on my shoulder.

"That's Argentina for you," Hugo said, smiling as if he knew precisely what I was thinking. "As for the meaning of 'cambalache,'" he concluded with a snort, "don't worry. If you live here long enough, I'm sure you'll figure it out on your own."

OH MY GOD, IT'S HOT!" THE TAXI DRIVER MOANED, FURIOUSLY rolling down his window. An oppressive wind shot through the car as we flew down Avenida Corrientes, Buenos Aires' Broadway. The blinking red, pink, and orange neon lights from the theaters made the heat even more intolerable. Girls in tank tops and high heels sauntered slowly down the sidewalk, their shoulders drooped.

"Can you believe how hot it is? So hot. The Argentines invented the *sensacion termica*, the 'heat index,' did you know that?"

"I don't think that's true." I mumbled.

". . . because it's hotter here than anywhere else in the world. In another city, in another life, perhaps, we could go swim in the river and cool off. But this isn't the Río de la Plata, it's the Río de la *Mierda*. You stick your finger in the river, your finger melts off because of all the acid, the pollution! You know why it's so dirty, the river? Because there's so much corruption in this country. I heard that, soon, there won't even be any fresh water left to wash dishes. . . . "

"That doesn't sound true either."

"Maybe not, maybe not. But, still, my God, couldn't we could get somebody else to come here and clean the river up? Aren't there some Dutch dudes who could come and do it for us? Now, there's a country that knows what they're doing! Come on, there *must* be at least one or two Dutchmen out there who are unemployed. Couldn't they just make a quick trip to poor Argentina to help us out? They come, a pipe or two and *listo*, problem solved."

"I think it's the French who run the water company here."

"No, no, *not* the French," the cabbie protested, clicking his tongue. "They're Latin like us. That's the problem. That's why everything here is so *complicado*. What we need is a serious country like the Dutch. It's not like here. But they would probably never come to Argentina, eh? They think we're all clowns here, eh, don't they? It's so hot, oh my God. . . . "

A CROSS THE AISLE FROM ME ON THE PLANE RIDE DOWN, there was a pasty middle-aged American man dressed in full jungle regalia: khaki shorts, multi-zippered fishing vest, comically large mud boots, and a wide-brimmed camouflage hat borrowed straight from Dr. Livingston himself. I wouldn't have been surprised to learn he kept a mosquito net in his carry-on—right next to his bullwhip and kerosene torch. About half an hour before we touched down, he began slathering sunscreen all over his body; the sweet odor of coconut mingled awkwardly with that of the soggy microwaved croissants that the flight attendants were beginning to slam about at the rear of the cabin. The man began sweating profusely the moment the plane landed, apparently steeling himself for the Amazon blast furnace that surely lurked outside.

I had left my Indiana Jones outfit at home, but the truth was that I felt just as foolish upon my arrival as that man must have. Nothing could have ever prepared me for Buenos Aires. I had gone expecting standard-issue Latin America— jungles, spicy food, glittering beaches, diarrhea—and was shocked to find what appeared to be a glittering oasis of European civilization at the end of the world. Entire neighborhoods of finely wrought mansions looked to be lifted straight from Paris. Majestic trees with blooming purple and red flowers lined the wide city streets that were laid out on a perfect grid. Dark, handsome men in cardigan sweaters or cream-colored suits dashed briskly through the happy hum of downtown pedestrian malls, chattering away on their mobile phones, pushing to close a deal. Cafés buzzed with feverish debates on French literature, Cuban politics or, more frequently, Argentine economics. There was no spicy food to be found. (Argentines detest it, claiming that it takes the "real" taste away from food. I would later meet locals who found ranch dressing "too hot.") At most restaurants, the menu consisted entirely of pasta, beef, and more beef. There was no beach, there were four seasons, the snakes were harmless, and you could leave your malaria pills at home. For someone like me who had believed that everything south of the U.S. border more or less resembled Tijuana, Buenos Aires was an utter revelation. You could even drink the water!

The city's wealth and sophistication had been sneaking up on unsuspecting travelers for decades. "Buenos Aires is something between Paris and New York," declared James Bryce, a British diplomat and writer. "It has the business rush and the luxury of the one, the gaiety and pleasure-loving aspect of the other. Everybody seems to have money, and to like spending it, and to like letting everybody else know that it is being spent. . . . Loitering in the great Avenida de Mayo and watching the hurrying crowd and the whirl of motor cars, and the gay shop-windows, and the open-air cafés on the sidewalks, and the Parisian glitter of the women's dresses, one feels much nearer to Europe than anywhere else in South America. . . . Nowhere else in the world does one get a stronger impression of exuberant wealth and extravagance."

Oh, sure—I had heard the rumors, the grumblings of the taxi drivers and the peddlers of Marxist propaganda. It was said that Buenos Aires had fallen on hard times. Bryce described the city as he saw it in 1912, and some of the sheen had obviously come off in the decades since. Many of those Parisian mansions were now missing windows—some were occupied by dozens of squatter families, and others were collapsing after decades of apparent neglect. But surely this was temporary—those who complained were merely the inevitable "losers" of globalization that I had learned about in college. In fact, there was good reason to believe that Argentina, just like the countries of the old Eastern bloc, was on the verge of an epic awakening. Spain had also undergone such a transformation—*la marcha*, they called it—during the 1980s, when democracy and capitalism made decades of decay under Franco simply melt away. In Madrid, I had met a grizzled old Brit who had lived through the whole thing and deemed it the greatest time of his life. "It happened almost overnight," he recalled. "All of a sudden, you saw these tall, busty teenage girls walking down the street in mini-skirts and go-go boots, arm-in-arm with their shriveled little grandmothers in wool shawls. You could see the transformation right there in front of you. The parties, the booze . . . and, my God, the sex. Everybody was having sex with everybody. If you *ever* get a chance to live through something similar," he implored me, his cheeks blushing with the memory, "grab onto that place and don't let go." So I bought myself a 36-pack of Argentine, Prime-brand condoms and pronounced myself ready for the coming revolution.

I wasn't finding a job quite as quickly as I had anticipated—a momentary setback, I reassured myself—so I took to wandering about Buenos Aires for hours at a time, a stranger in a strange city. I would wake up every morning at exactly 8

A.M. (I had a slick new alarm clock), nibble on a few crackers (Argentines spurned breakfast entirely), pick a direction (usually south, God knows why), and walk. Nobody knew who I was. Nobody cared. I could have set myself on fire, and that would have been the end of it; my poor parents would have received an indecipherable letter and a box of ashes a few weeks later. I realized that, for the first time in my life, I was completely on my own.

I was on a self-mandated budget of seventy pesos a week—equivalent to seventy U.S. dollars, just enough to afford ham sandwiches every day for lunch and a ticket to the movies on Friday. Buenos Aires was still very pricey (twenty-first on the annual ranking of the 150 most expensive world capitals, on a par with Paris and Washington, D.C.). More than other places, this was a city where you really needed money to entertain yourself. There were no beaches, no great museums; there was only the street. So I decided to embrace my status as an anonymous derelict and really explore the place, every last alley. If I saw an interesting-looking street, I would walk down it; if I saw an open door, I would enter. And at the end of a particularly constructive day, I would reward myself with a cheap but delicious Argentine steak for dinner.

One afternoon, I discovered a cluster of antique bookstores in the basement of a shopping center on Calle Florida, the main shopping thoroughfare downtown. There seemed to be a citywide fire sale underway on anything antique—I couldn't understand how the prices could possibly be so low—so, without causing irreparable damage to my budget, I was able to begin collecting works by Bryce and others among the select fraternity of travelers who had uncovered some of the secrets to this weird and wonderful place.

One of them, Burton Holmes, had been a veteran globe-trotter around the turn of the twentieth century who had coined the term "travelogue" and had a Hollywood star to show for it. And even he had been shocked by what he found in Argentina. "We go to Europe or to the Orient to see what we expect to see," he wrote. "We go prepared—our education, our reading, the oft-related experiences of our friends, have made the atmosphere of Europe, and even the Orient, so familiar to us that we are robbed of all sensations of surprise or novelty when we find ourselves in celebrated places and come face to face with famous sights. It is all as we expect to find it. South America, on the contrary, offers us the thrill of the unexpected that makes us experience the sensation of discovery. Every North American who lands in Buenos Aires feels like a modern Christopher Columbus: he has discovered not a new continent but something vastly more amazing—a great city."

This was exactly how I felt, as if Argentina was some kind of intimate secret. I was particularly drawn to books that would help me avoid repeating the mistakes of the stereo-typical ignorant American abroad. So I read with great inter-est an account by Hudson Strode, an English professor from the University of Alabama. Strode had visited Argentina dur-ing the 1930s and written a lightly fictionalized account where one of the main characters meets an Argentine man born to American parents. The Argentine rages against his guests, berating them for their lack of knowledge. "Some of your Americans have the idea that we're nothing but a lot of feathered Indians," he protested. "You pretend to be greatly amazed that we have motor cars and don't ride wild horses into the shops. You think that life here consists of revolutions and tangos."

Revolutions and tangos? I read this and felt a sharp pang of nostalgia—either one might have been fun to experience, I mused. But these were both things from Argentina's past, surely. In a country that was optimistically looking toward a bright future, there was no room for either.

I THINK YOU'VE CHOSEN THE RIGHT PLACE," THE AMERICAN pilot was saying between shots of bourbon, "although I haven't really heard of anybody getting jobs here. I think the job market is kind of flat right now. Yeah, that's what I've heard. I'm sure things'll work out for you though. You had the fuckin' *cojones* to get on that plane. Now you're here, and everything'll work itself out. You'll be great, you'll see."

It was my first Saturday night in Buenos Aires and, rather than spend it alone, I had opted to go out. Bars seemed to be in short supply—there were two cafés on every corner, but for an American-style bar or even an Irish pub, the pickings were slim. I flipped through my Lonely Planet guide and found Henry J. Bean's, a counterfeit T.G.I. Friday's with American street-signs and stoplights on the wall and menus in broken English. I felt a bit embarrassed to be there, but I simply didn't know where else to go. I had never even been to a bar by myself—I always had friends to go out with back home—and I had neglected to read the "lonely guy at bar" etiquette manual for Americans, much less the Argentine version. After an hour spent carefully examining every STOP and YIELD sign in the joint, I (very painfully) struck up a conversation with a somewhat older, equally hapless-looking American (I would later learn that Henry J. Bean's basically depended on them to stay in business) who earned a living by flying charters all over the world for wealthy businessmen and managed to use phrases like "fuckin' cojones" without any apparent inhibition. He drank a rather disturbing amount for a pilot.

"You like this country?" the pilot asked.

"I think so."

"That's refreshing," he said, "because everybody else in Latin America *despises* these motherfuckers. They think the Argentines are a bunch of arrogant pricks. And they're probably right! Then again, if you had a country like this. . . . "

"It's a beautiful place," I agreed.

"Damn straight!" he exclaimed. "They've had some bad governments over the years, a bad run, but I think Menem finally put them on the right track. People sure bitched enough about it—these people love to bitch, good God!—but no pain, no gain, I say. If people here are complaining about it, it's probably a good thing, you know?"

During a decade in power, Carlos Menem had managed to privatize not only the state telephone monopoly and the water company but also the post office, the pension system, and even the Argentine equivalent of the FCC. For his efforts, he had received the undying affection of the IMF, a $250,000 Ferrari Testarossa (a "gift" from Italian businessmen), plus a golf course, a spa, an artificial lake, and a tennis court for his new mansion back in La Rioja province. Most people refused to say his name out loud, believing it bad luck, so they referred to him as "Mendez" instead. (Argentines had a phobia about palindromes; plus, a famous local boating racer had once shaken Menem's hand and then lost his right arm in a spectacular accident.) Mendez had just left power two months before, but he was already plotting a comeback and was engaged to marry a former Miss Universe from Chile. Nobody could quite figure out what had happened to all the money from the privatizations.

"Hey," I said. "Do you know what the word 'cambalache' means?"

"No idea."

The house band was playing Huey Lewis and the News. "Hip to Be Square" actually sounded better when sung with an Argentine accent.

"What do you think of the girls here?" I asked.

"Total waste of time!" he shouted, slamming down his glass. He surveyed the room, methodically inspecting the asses—and only the asses—of every female within a 50-foot radius. "They're hot as hell, but impossible. Like talking to a brick wall. Frankly, I don't think anybody in this country ever gets laid. But I'll save you some time," he said, leaning in confidentially: "The escort services here—world class. The best I've seen."

"You mean. . . . "

"Of course! Goddamn, what are they feeding you boys down in Texas?" The pilot rolled his eyes and chuckled to himself and I suddenly realized, like a shot to the abdomen, that I profoundly disliked this man. "I'm going out and meeting a girl after this. All it would take is one phone call and, you know. . . . "

I shook my head no.

"Suit yourself," he said, slamming a $100 bill down on the bar. "Mark my words, though: You stay in this country long enough, and you'll change your mind. When you do, remember your old American friend you met at the bar—and give that ho a little tap on the ass for me!" He laughed and turned to head out the door. "Seriously though, man, good luck in Argentina. You'll be a big success. Things here are going to be just fine."

THEN, ONE FINE SPRING OCTOBER AFTERNOON, THE VICE president quit.

There were two ways to hear news like this in Buenos Aires. One was from taxi drivers, who always knew about bond market crashes, coups, and Hollywood boob jobs long before anybody else. Now, this is somewhat true the world over, but in Argentina, the recent economic troubles had bestowed taxi drivers with a special cache. When an entire generation of Argentine middle managers was fired during Menem's "free-market" reforms of the 1990s, seemingly every middle-aged man in the city used his severance pay to buy a cab. Accountants and lawyers who should have been in the prime of their careers were now left to troll the city all day in vain—and Buenos Aires rapidly became a city of taxi drivers with no passengers. I had cabbies who had been country managers for Chase Manhattan, factory heads for Ford, pilots for Aerolineas Argentinas. To keep their minds sharp, they listened to news radio all day. "Can you believe the rate on the thirty-day Treasury bill today?" they would ask with the same tone that cab drivers in most other countries discussed the weather. "9.76 percent! And with the Federal Reserve in *your* country just having cut rates by 25 basis points last week! This madness can't go on much longer. . . . "

The other real-time information source was Crónica TV, perhaps the ultimate only-in-Argentina institution. It was just one of four twenty-four-hour, live-action channels that sought to satisfy Argentines' insatiable appetite for news about themselves, but Crónica had somehow perfected a uniquely local mix of irony, bloodlust, and narcissism. Before each cut-away live shot, the screen went bright red, with cartoonish white block letters blaring the news: HORRIBLE MURDER IN BELGRANO or DISGRACE: NEW SCANDAL IN CONGRESS. For reasons I could never quite decipher, an anchor read each headline aloud to a rousing marching-band rendition of "Stars and Stripes Forever." My Argentine friends would later assure me this was meant to be deeply hilarious, just like some of Crónica's more inspired headlines: GOOD EXAMPLE IN CHINA: SENATOR EXECUTED FOR CORRUPTION or DRUNK DRIVER ALMOST PROVOKES TRAGEDY; BATMAN ONLY WITNESS. Amid all this, if something *genuinely* important was going on—a fatal bus wreck, for instance, or a late-night budget debate in Congress—Crónica could always be counted on to have a camera there, broadcasting live. And for an hour starting at 5 P.M. every day, without further explanation, two furry hand puppets took their place behind the anchor's desk and delivered the news.

As it happened, this particular day was a classic Crónica day. I was walking by a café downtown when I saw lots of men standing around, gaping at the TV, grasping their bald spots, busily gesticulating and gossiping among themselves. I craned my neck and saw the signature white block letters on the red screen: CHACHO IS GONE.

Carlos "Chacho" Alvarez needed ten months as vice president to discover what all his compatriots already knew: Argentine politics was a dirty game. There had been a bribery scandal in the Senate; it hadn't seemed at all extraordinary— "This is how things were always done," a mystified senator would say later—but for whatever reason, Chacho had become indignant and had a falling-out with the president. Newspapers said the two men had stopped speaking to each other weeks ago. Even in Argentina, where bitter personal rivalries grew faster than cash crops, such a standoff was untenable.

Crónica cut away to camera #5, which was of course already on the scene outside Chacho's apartment in Barrio Norte. A crowd of hundreds had magically materialized. The onlookers screamed and wailed in despair as the camera rolled. "Don't go! Don't go!" yelled one old lady, sobbing and pleading as she stared straight into the camera. Others had come prepared with handmade signs. "God save the country," one said. "Don't take away our dreams," read another.

As the sun set, Chacho held a press conference at a downtown hotel. All four TV news stations turned out for this one. Tears welled up in his eyes as he softly explained his reasons for quitting. "It makes me ashamed that a youth of sixteen or seventeen years old feels that politics is a synonym of crime," he declared, his voice trembling. "You're either for the old way of doing things, which has to die, or you leave, and then you fight for a new way, which this crisis should help reveal. My resignation is an act of loyalty."

When he finished his speech, Chacho rested his head on his wife's shoulder, an expression of complete loss and despair etched on his face. Flashbulbs exploded like it was a Milan fashion show. And at that moment, you could see the faintest trace of a smile on Chacho's face—as if, somewhere, not far beneath the surface, he was secretly enjoying all the drama.

Two hours later, the rapidly graying President Fernando de la Rúa, looking dapper and almost competent in his signature navy-blue blazer and ascot, urgently addressed the nation on television from the Casa Rosada, the Pink House. "I'm going to fight until the end of all battles," De la Rúa vowed, his eyebrow twitching, a barely detectable slur in his speech. "There is no crisis here."

Naturally, that was the day the crisis *really* started.

AS THE STOCK MARKET CRASHED, OLD LADIES ATTACKED politicians with umbrellas, street demonstrations paralyzed traffic, shops closed their doors forever, cafés emptied out, and rumors swirled of a coup, I started wondering if maybe, just maybe, I was a complete and total idiot.

It dawned on me that, hmm, perhaps a country with an unemployment rate of 20 percent (and soaring higher by the day) wasn't such a fabulous place to look for my first job out of college. I had quickly given up on my initial hope of working for the city's 125-year-old English-language newspaper, the *Buenos Aires Herald*—no jobs there although, after much haggling, they did offer to let me work for free. American multinationals with offices in Buenos Aires hadn't just stopped hiring; they were leaving the country altogether. Even my foolproof backup plan of teaching English was looking doomed. I discovered that the English-language schools of Buenos Aires were largely staffed by second- and third-generation Anglo-Argentines, descendants of British tycoons who had built Argentina's railroads a century before and lived in perfect Tudor mansions in suburbs with names like Temperley and Hurlingham. Most modern-day Anglo-Argentines no longer took their tea at 4 P.M., had seen London only on TV, and often spoke with insufferably atrocious grammar, but their accents still miraculously mimicked the clipped English of the 1920s that their great-grandfathers had once spoken, as if a linguistic moment had been frozen in time. "So sorry, old chap," a sandy-haired, freckly school headmaster told me, "but you've got the wrong accent to teach here. In Argentina, we speak *Brit*-ish English, don't you know. Of course, nobody has any money for English classes these days anyhow. Best of luck, cheerio!"

There were other problems. Contrary to my expectations, the language was proving to be one of them. The *porteños*—literally "people of the port," as residents of Buenos Aires called themselves—spoke a bizarre dialect that was radically different from standard Castilian Spanish; all conversations I overheard sounded like arguments among Sicilian mafiosos who were on the verge of gunning each other down. Both the pronunciation and the syntax bore little resemblance to what I'd learned in Spain, as I discovered to my great dismay when, seeking directions to the bus stop, I asked an elderly woman: "*¿Dónde puedo coger el autobús?*" which, in Argentine Spanish, means: "Where can I fuck the bus?"

The woman looked at me grimly but without surprise, as if she had heard this error before. "We don't say that here," she said gently, and then she personally escorted me two blocks away to the bus stop.

I was tired of spending endless days walking around the city, but mostly I was tired of making an ass out of myself every time I opened my mouth, so, with the patient old lady's assistance, I began whiling away the hours in blissful silence by riding the famous #60 city bus. (In Argentina, even the buses are celebrities, probably because they are reputed to be a local invention. In the years to come I would hear, with wildly varying degrees of accuracy, that Argentines also invented the ballpoint pen, Thousand Island dressing—known locally as "golf sauce"—heart bypass surgery, psycho-analysis, and, yes, the heat index.) The #60 ran from one extreme of the city to the other, was immaculately clean, and kept its windows open for a nice breeze. Every ten minutes or so, a vendor would climb aboard and sell comic books, candy, bubble gum, or a deck of cards. In sum, the #60 bus deserved its fame—it offered the best, most luxurious, and most unapologetically antisocial tour of Buenos Aires that could be had for just seventy centavos.

The bus departed every two minutes from the old Victorian train station known as Constitución, from which trains had once clattered all the way to the lake district of Patagonia, with its trout fishing and ski resorts. No more. There had been a luxurious restaurant inside the station—"five forks," as Argentines called their finest dining establishments. But now the restaurant was gone, replaced by shoe-shiners and pickpockets and the occasional hot dog vendor. From Constitución, the #60 passed within spitting distance (quite a few Argentines took this literally) of the Congreso, an unnecessarily elaborate imitation of the U.S. Capitol with a green, 250-foot copper dome. It was completed in 1906 at a cost more than twice its original budget—a clear precedent for the years to come. Across the street was a sculpture garden with a fountain that had long ago run dry; the sculpture, of a young man holding an oar, was laced with graffiti. 30,000 DISAPPEARED, read one inscription, scrawled in crude black letters. WE WILL NEITHER FORGET NOR FORGIVE.

The bus then flew down Avenida Callao toward Recoleta, the old-money neighborhood in a city of nothing but old money. Somewhere along this half-mile stretch, something like South America melted away into something like Europe: the buildings became more exuberant and more carefully crafted, and instead of empty façades, the entire structures were ornate and chiseled. Every three blocks there seemed to be another fine cheese and wine store owned by the Al Queso, Queso chain—which told you as much about a neighborhood in Buenos Aires as a Starbucks did in the U.S.A. Dramatic spires and sculptures crowned every corner. But just as I was lulled into thinking this might be the "Paris of South America" that James Bryce and Burton Holmes had so fondly described, the bus violently lurched left and rumbled up Avenida Las Heras, a gridlocked canyon of blue smoke and haze. The deafening roar of decrepit bus engines and honking taxis mingled with bookstores, newspaper stands, and professional dog-walkers. The bus passed in front of a half-finished neo-Gothic building with two giant holes where its two spires should have been, as if the builders had simply run out of money; someone with a healthy sense of irony had turned this structure into the College of Engineering for the University of Buenos Aires.

Farther north, on the left, there was the unremarkable Parque Las Heras—a forest of undernourished trees and cracked sidewalks—which, despite its privileged perch in the posh half of the city, had the rotten luck of being constructed in the 1960s, when grand things were no longer being built in Argentina. The park had been erected on the wreckage of an old prison, which was now commemorated only by a sunken plaque; "Here in 1956 was the massacre of. . . ." After passing within three blocks of my apartment, the #60 bus slowly snaked its way past the notorious Villa 31 shantytown, through the prosperous northern suburbs of Nunez and Vicente Lopez; picked up speed as it passed the walled estates and tinted windows of San Isidro; and then chugged in to its final destination of El Tigre (no relation whatsoever to the dancer), the muddy river delta and one-time playground for the rich where I could still see signs for English rowing clubs, long since closed. Just a few hundred meters offshore, I could see giant barges out on the Rio de la Plata carrying the soy and wheat that had as recently as the 1930s made Argentina one of the five richest countries in the world.

Those days were gone, and it appeared that they were never coming back. It was now (very belatedly) obvious to me that the problems here predated Chacho and even my lifetime. Argentina had been on a hopeless, seemingly irreversible seventy-year losing streak—it was like the Chicago

Cubs of countries. It had begun the century with a higher per capita income than Sweden or Spain, and on par with Germany. Perhaps no other nation had fallen so far, so fast. Yet there had been no devastating wars, no epic plagues, floods, or droughts. There had been no one tyrant, no Idi Amin or Josef Stalin who had single-handedly run the place into the ground. A country blessed with some of the earth's richest farmland was now having problems feeding its people. And while the world is full of countries with abundant natural resources that have failed to reach their potential, perhaps none of them also possess Argentina's wealth of human capital: a vibrant and skilled population that is nearly 100 percent literate. Despite all this, the country was stuck in a death spiral. It seemed that things were about to get dramatically worse. And nobody quite understood why.

I would usually wander about El Tigre for a few hours, my head spinning. Why I had hitched my fortunes to such a country? What kind of fool would have left behind the greatest economic expansion in U.S. history to come to a place like this? How would I ever explain my impending failure to my friends and family? Was this "adventure"? Then, I would board the train back downtown. We would reach the station, the crowd would mill busily about, and these questions would slowly dissipate from my mind . . . until one day, when I saw a table of CDs for sale at the street market outside Retiro with all the chirping alarm clocks and, on a whim, hoping to maybe find some clues to this riddle of a country, I bought a pirated two-peso recording of "Cambalache."

THE WORD, LITERALLY TRANSLATED, MEANS "JUNK SHOP." I had to buy an extra-thick Spanish-to-English dictionary to figure this out; "cambalache" wasn't traditional Spanish, of course, but a word from sixteenth-century Portuguese that had somehow made it into the *lunfardo* slang that was common in Buenos Aires and, thus, the tango. Lunfardo also contained words from Italian (Genovese, Neopolitan, and seemingly everywhere else), French, and some English. It was like a language within a language that seemed specifically designed to bewilder outsiders like myself.

More specifically, a cambalache is a place where stolen goods are resold—an illicit market, what some would call a fence—so, in essence, this Argentine "national anthem" was calling the entire twentieth century one giant rip-off:

> *Today it is the same*
> *Whether you're decent or a traitor!*
> *Ignorant, a genius, a crook,*
> *Generous or a scam artist!*
> *Everything is the same! Nothing is better!*
> *An ass is the same*
> *As a great professor!*

Something deep inside of me still recoiled, like some kind of gag reflex, when I heard such thick, unvarnished cynicism. Yet, I found that with each passing day I spent in Buenos Aires, the less ridiculous the lyrics seemed.

I was getting no phone calls back from the English-teaching institutes. My allotted budget had trickled down to near nothing, so I couldn't go out to meet people, and (for the

moment, anyway) I sure as hell wasn't ready to call any escort services. My self-guided bus tours and walkabouts had
come to an end. So I became horribly, comically, withdrawn.
I spent hours flushing the toilet over and over to see if the
water really went down the pipes backward. (I could never
quite tell.) I took to watching TV for hours at a time. One afternoon, I stumbled across a Chilean cable channel that was
showing a live broadcast of the inauguration of their new
president. I watched the entire thing, all four hours, including the military parades and the president's speech. And
when the event was finally over, I was overcome by a deep,
despairing sadness.

I think that was the moment when I decided that I either
needed to get a life, or go back home to Texas.

Desperate, I called one of the two phone numbers I had
brought with me to Argentina. I was house-sitting for an
Argentine friend of mine who was working as an advertising
executive in New York; the number was for her father, Carlos. He was in his fifties, a widower twice over, and had met
his current girlfriend during a tango lesson. Carlos had been
offering to take me to a *milonga*—a place where tangos are
danced—since the first day I arrived. I had always politely
declined, trying not to roll my eyes.

But now. . . .

"If you're free, Mónica and I are going on Thursday night
to the Niño Bien, a traditional old club near Congreso. We'll
try to get there early, around 1 A.M. You're welcome to come.
We can reserve a table for three, right by the dance floor.
There will be girls there."

This should have been enough, but I still balked.

"Thanks, Carlos," I replied. "We'll see. I'll call you later this week. I might have some plans on Thursday."

Yet, the next night, I listened to the rest of the CD, apparently a kind of "Greatest Hits of the Tango," and was surprised to find the compilation intriguing. The melodies were delicate, well-orchestrated, and unique. Not all of the songs were as acidic and over-the-top as "Cambalache." Most of them did seem to center on nostalgia and loss, but these easily exaggerated emotions were often conveyed with lyrics that were genuinely moving and even subtle. A few of the songs—particularly one named "Volver" (To Return), performed by the famous tango singer Carlos Gardel—I could even identify with:

> *I'm afraid of the nights*
> *That, populated with memories,*
> *Light up my dreams.*
> *But the traveler who flees*
> *Sooner or later settles down. . . .*
> *And although I didn't want to return,*
> *You always come back to your first love.*
> *The still street where the echo said:*
> *"Your life is yours, your love is yours."*
> *Under the teasing gaze of the stars*
> *That with indifference today see me return.*

That same night, I called Carlos back.

"I'll see you on Thursday," I sighed. "Should I wear a suit?"

My TAXI ROLLED UP OUTSIDE THE NIÑO BIEN JUST AFTER
1 A.M. The club was a few blocks away from Constitución in
a faded part of town, decaying even by Buenos Aires standards, but with crumbling balconies and roofs overgrown
with weeds and tiny anarchic tree shoots growing in the
cracks. There seemed to be no light here, only shadows. A
sole *cartonero* wheeled his wooden cart down the sidewalk,
balancing a stack of yesterday's newspapers and whistling
off-key. Down by the corner, two prostitutes in red dresses
stood patiently, waiting for business they knew would come.
I paid the cabbie, pulled tight the shoelaces on my tennis
shoes, grimy and worn from so much traipsing about, and
walked upstairs to the second floor.

I turned the corner into a blinding white light and realized
that I hadn't *touched* anyone in a month.

Here before me was a sea of people, all locked in an intimate embrace. There were about two hundred people dancing, slowly rotating around the room, two by two, as if on a
grand carousel. The men stood up straight, their chests puffed
out, their arms encircling the women protectively. The
women leaned in ever so slightly, pressing their chests tightly
up against their partners', their legs lightly tracing figure-
eights on the hardwood dance floor. Around the periphery sat
dozens of tables, where a smiling crowd gesticulated madly
and laughed at each other's jokes. A warm buzz of happy conversation echoed through the hall. Waitresses in low-cut
black dresses carried trays with glasses of scotch and espressos, smiling flirtatiously and sneaking furtive glances at the
best dancers in the room.

I scanned the room, dizzy again with the unique sensation of having discovered something completely new and unexpected. I thought again of the poor American with the mosquito net; every preconception I had about the tango was instantly and completely inverted. There were no kicks, no acrobatics, no roses in clenched teeth. Instead, there were only incremental movements, bodies rubbing up against each other. It immediately struck me as the most civilized place in the world.

"So what do you think?" Carlos asked.

"Shouldn't they be dancing cheek to cheek?" I asked.

Carlos looked at me like I had lost my mind. Then he realized what I meant and laughed. "Don't be ridiculous," he said. "That step is called the *salida americana*. They invented that just for Hollywood. Nobody does it in real life."

I could see why they had felt it necessary to dramatize the tango for the movies; as seen here, the movements might have been too understated, too incremental to convey real drama on the big screen. But the understatement, the subtlety of the real thing in person made it much more intimate—and infinitely more sexy.

We sat down.

"Good crowd tonight," Carlos observed. "Many of the legends are here."

I didn't know anything about any legends, and of course I had never seen the tango in person before, but it was clear to me from the beginning how to distinguish the pros from the amateurs: if a couple danced particularly well, the woman would close her eyes and smile. This was more remarkable than it might seem; the dance floor was jam-packed with people, making each movement fraught with peril. Though there were no Broadway-style kicks, there *were* quite a lot of high heels flying around, and bodies twisting with no rhyme or reason that I could decipher. The apparent anarchy of the tango made things doubly dangerous; there seemed to be no set pattern, no orderly circle as with the waltz. Collision seemed imminent at every juncture. Indeed, all of the men had their eyes wide open; it was apparently their responsibility alone to avert disaster. Still, for a woman to dance with her eyes closed was a leap of faith, no doubt. I looked around and saw women from the age of fifteen to eighty-five, all shapes and sizes; the good ones, the ones who moved with the most fluidity and least effort, danced blindly, like the world around them had completely vanished.

The whole place was one big spectacle. The biggest show in the room, however, was not taking place out on the dance floor. One table over, on the edge of the twirling mass of people, a bald man in a cream-colored suit was holding court. Everyone at the Niño Bien was coming over to pay their respects. As soon as couples entered the room, they strolled over to his table and gave him a big, theatrical hug and kiss. Only then, it seemed, were they permitted to order a coffee or dance a tango. For his part, the bald man treated all the attention like he expected it—as if the mass adulation was not just routine but, in his mind, thoroughly warranted. He was notably handsome, perhaps fifty-five, and his large brown eyes rested comfortably on whomever came to pay their respects. He wore a black shirt, no tie, and had sleek gray hair. He was thin and well kept, perfectly contained. He had the unmistakable air of a judge, or a politician, or a Mafia don—or, this being Argentina, perhaps some combination of the three.

"Is that the owner?" I asked Carlos.

Carlos craned his neck. "No, that's not the owner. I don't know who that guy is. He looks like an actor."

"Why is everybody going over to see him?"

"Maybe he's The Godfather," Carlos said with a wink. "Go kiss his ring."

Without further ado, Carlos and Mónica stood up from the table. He took her softly by the hand and led her to the dance floor. Then, ever so delicately, he drew her into his arms; they began to dance, and she closed her eyes and smiled. It seemed that Carlos was, in fact, a pro.

"I see the tango hasn't entered your soul yet."

It was The Godfather, leaning over from his table, grinning at me. By now, I had been in Argentina long enough that I was only slightly fazed when random people struck up conversations with me.

"How can you tell?" I asked, smiling back.

"Because if it had," The Godfather replied, "you'd be out there dancing."

"Oh." I laughed. "You're probably right."

"You're new. Would you like to have a coffee?"

Somewhat bewildered, I nodded yes and sidled over to his table.

The waitress came over right away with a smile, something that happens in Argentina with the frequency of a lunar eclipse. We had our espressos in about thirty seconds—"Extra strong, sir, just for you," the waitress cooed—and I felt like I had just stepped into a vastly different, parallel world far superior to my own.

"Where are you from?" The Godfather asked.

"Texas."

"Ah, Texas," he repeated with a fond smile. "Home of the cowboy, cousin of the *gaucho*. And what are you doing in Argentina?"

"Well," I said, "I guess I'm living here."

"For how long?"

"We'll see."

"How strange," he replied. "I didn't realize immigrants still came to Argentina. My grandfather came from Naples in 1905, worked as a tailor, didn't sleep for thirty years. That generation worked like beasts, I tell you. But the family prospered, and we stayed. I doubt it's so easy today, though. Are you having any success?"

"Not yet."

"Hm, that's a shame. So are you going to learn the tango?"

"You're the second person to ask me that," I said. "I don't know yet. I guess I'm thinking about it."

"It's a decision you have to make on your own," The Godfather said, nodding empathetically. He settled into his chair and took a short sip from his espresso, surveying the room. "When I was a boy, we treated the milonga like it was a church; we went every Saturday night, religiously, with enormous devotion. There was a very famous tango club we attended called Sin Rumbo. That's where we usually went. We danced for fun, of course; that's all we had. We were amateurs. We didn't know a thing about shows or technique. These young *pibes* today, these guys who tour the world, they are infinitely more intelligent than we were. They're making a fortune off this thing. That didn't occur to us.

"But—look, I don't want to sound like an old geezer here, *un viejo choto*, but I will say this—The tango was much more dramatic for us. We didn't make money, but the stakes were elevated, you know? If the milonga was on a Saturday night, you'd start preparing around noon." A dreamy smile spread across his face. "Your mother would iron your shirt for you, and lay it out on your bed. You'd go to the barber, and they would trim your hair, and massage your cheeks."

"Why massage the cheeks?" I asked, intrigued.

"So you'd look better," he answered reflexively, dismissively. Then he paused, as if suddenly aware of his own bullshit, and he burst into laughter, throwing up his hands in defeat. "Oh, I don't know!" he exclaimed. "It was all in your head. If you don't feel handsome, then you don't look handsome. So they massaged your cheeks. Who knows why? But, I tell you, it worked!

"We would all meet at a friend's house and drink coffee and comb our hair and make conspiracies about which girls we were going to conquer that night. And then, at the set hour, we'd get on a bus to the club." His voice lowered to a whisper, and he leaned across the table toward me, letting me in on a secret. "The closer you got to the club, the more you started to sweat. Then, three or four blocks from the milonga, you'd hear the music, the *bandoneon* and the guitar echoing in the night, and your heart would pound, *ba-dum, ba-dum, ba-dum.*

"You'd walk in, and light your cigarette, and put on your best *cara de malevo*, your best villain's face. Your heart was still pounding, but of course you'd have to hide it from the girls. And you'd dance, and after one or two tangos you'd finally relax a bit, and it was vivid and beautiful and soothing. But your heart never stopped pounding. And it never has. I still get that rush from the tango. I still do, I swear to the Virgin Mary."

At that moment, some young girls entering the club walked over and kissed The Godfather on the cheek. He graciously smiled, and then he watched them intently as they walked away.

"Plus," he added, "the girls have nice asses."

"That's important," I said, laughing.

"Very important," he replied. And then he turned abruptly serious. "Can you believe they tried to take the tango away from us? Can you fathom how unbelievably stupid that was? All these girls, this wonderful music, how are you going to take that away? Yet the *militares* and the priests wouldn't permit the tango. They tried to change the *lunfardo* for more sophisticated things. They wanted to make Argentina clean and orderly. So you couldn't have tangos about catching your wife, murdering her lover, and then fucking somebody else. The church didn't want that; it wasn't 'proper.' Of course, the priests were busy fucking little boys," he added with a dark snort of a laugh, "but we didn't know that back then, did we? Stupid us.

"The tango was the soul of Argentina. It was the voice of the people, and they couldn't take that away. They tried. And they almost succeeded. But they couldn't. When you go to another country, you look for the soul of the country, for the roots. That's what this is. So, in that sense, congratulations— you've already done better than most travelers in discovering *de qué se trata este pais*, what this country is all about.

"Some of this has faded, of course. These clubs, places like Sunderland, places like the Niño Bien," he said, surveying the room, "these are the only ones left. The cultural activity in this country used to be spectacular. Orchestras, people playing cards, dancing all night. That has gone away now. Now, a place like Niño Bien is just the basics. It's pure tango, that's all. I just have enormous respect for the dance. I take it as a kind of catharsis. This is a very passionate thing. I go to the milonga," he said, sticking his arm out, feigning dancing, "and I listen to my wife's heartbeat while I dance."

I sat there silently, awed by this astounding success of a man. But I still hadn't figured out exactly what caused him to be treated like such royalty by the crowd at the Niño Bien. He wasn't a famous tango dancer, and he wasn't a politician, so what was it? Why the adulation? Why was he apparently regarded as The Godfather?

I asked him what he did for a living.

"Salesman," he answered, innocently.

Had he ever toured the world dancing tango?

"No, I never taught a class, and I never did a show. I just have tremendous respect for the dance."

I asked him how old he was.

"I'm sixty-eight years old," he said with a smile. "Do I look it?"

"No," I replied, genuinely stunned. "I'd have given you ten years less."

He laughed, pleased with me—but mostly with himself.

"No, really," I insisted. "No bullshit. I'm serious."

"It's okay," he replied, sitting up straight and rearranging his collar. "I believe you. I take care of myself. I deserve it."

At that point, I surrendered. I gave up trying to figure out the mystery and decided to just relax and enjoy the company of someone who had lived a full, satisfying, charmed life.

"Well," I said, "do you have any advice for a young American who is considering trying to learn the tango?"

This had been intended as a throwaway question, an af-terthought. But now, The Godfather's smile broadened, he leaned back in his chair, and he regarded me with sudden respect. "How sweet," he muttered, almost to himself. "How marvelous." His gaze shifted away for a moment, deep in thought, and then he focused back on me, very serious.

"Fall in love, fall in love. That's my only advice. It can be with a girl, or with the music, or with the dance. It doesn't matter. But, whatever you do, fall in love. And, if you do this, then the tango, with all the bullshit that you'll go through along the way, will have been worth it for you."

With that, he stood up, shook my hand good-bye, and went to go listen to the heartbeat of his wife.

As DAWN BROKE, I STOOD OUT ON THE BALCONY OF THE Niño Bien, drinking scotch for the very first time and strug-gling like hell to keep it down. I had spent the remainder of the night at the table watching the dancers and drinking with reckless abandon. Carlos and Mónica were still out on the dance floor, lost in the music and the crowd and their own little world. I was exhausted, but happy.

Luis, the owner of the Niño Bien, was out there on the pa-tio with me, surveying the street with apparent satisfaction and sipping a café con leche. The same two prostitutes were standing on the corner below us, looking somewhat bewil-dered to still be there, alone.

"The crisis is affecting them, too," Luis whispered, pointing. "When they suffer, you know the rest of us are in real trouble."

We both snickered. At that moment, though, I felt the first real, sinking conviction in my heart that Argentina could be in for a worse fate than I could imagine.

"First time to the milonga?" Luis asked.

I nodded.

"*¿Y cómo te fue?*"

"Oh, I don't dance," I replied.

Luis scratched his head, frowned, and contemplated this for a moment. "You don't dance the tango?" he asked, one eyebrow arched. "Or you don't dance at all?"

"I'm not a dancer," I said.

"That's a shame," he replied, discreet but sincere. He leaned over the railing, looked back at me, and grinned. "You know, these are weird people. . . . "

I started to laugh. Then, we were both cracking up.

". . . No, really, it's true," Luis continued, still laughing. "These people are *weird*. I love them more than anyone, but they're unique, and as a foreigner you should know that these aren't typical Argentines; they're a species apart. These are the same people who kept the tango alive for so many years during the dark ages, when it almost disappeared. And now, Argentina is hurting, and people are looking for something that is ours again, and here we are. Isn't it odd that, just as the country endures its most terrible crisis, that people are rediscovering the tango? Why do you think that is?"

"I don't know," I replied. "Is that true?"

"Without a doubt," Luis said. "Business is booming. Not just for me but at all the milongas, it's the same thing. Every other business in Argentina is going bankrupt and closing its doors forever, but we're living *una epoca de oro*, a golden age. I have no idea why. But I think all of us owe these people a debt of gratitude."

"Do any of them give tango lessons?" I asked.

"Are you kidding?" Luis replied. "Each one of these old guys thinks he's the best tango dancer in the world. Any of them will give you a lesson if you ask them. I'll introduce you to a few if you want."

"That would be marvelous."

"Hmm, let's see. You can start with that guy over there, at the table with the young lady," Luis said, pointing back inside. "His name is Eduardo, and I know he has given classes to foreigners before. He dances like a filthy son of a bitch, but he knows what he's doing. You should talk to him first."

"Thank you."

Hours later, when the sun was fully up and my head was throbbing and I was leaving with Carlos and Mónica to go grab some coffee and churros for breakfast, I walked over to the table that Luis had indicated.

"Excuse me, sir," I said, tapping the hulking old sailor on the shoulder, "but I'm new to Argentina, and I want to learn how to tango."

part two

TEN STRAWBERRY DAIQUIRIS, PLEASE

THE FIRST THING YOU HAVE TO KNOW," EL TIGRE EXPLAINED, "is that in the tango, the man controls *everything*."

I grimaced. "Is that politically correct?"

"What does that mean?"

"Well. . . . "

"If you're not capable of leading a woman," El Tigre continued, unabated, "then you're wasting her time and yours. You could be Fred Astaire. It doesn't matter. The tango is not an athletic competition. It depends above all on your ability as a man to show the woman what to do, to guide her, to make her feel comfortable, to make her feel like a woman. That's what is really important."

"I see."

"Excellent. You're an exemplary student."

"So, is it time for me to go ask a woman to dance?"

"Fuck, no!" he snorted. "I have a reputation to protect, you know."

I was midway through my third lesson with El Tigre and, despite having plied him with over $100 worth of whiskey and a half-dozen bottles of cheap Malbec, the old son of a bitch hadn't let me dance with anybody yet. The only thing he would allow me to do was walk. Yes, walk. In a dark corner of the Confiteria Ideal, a tango café downtown that was the only place in Buenos Aires where it was possible to dance at 4 P.M. on a Monday (ah, the pleasures of unemployment!), El Tigre made me walk in circles, over and over and over. Everybody else in the room was dancing and having a grand time, but I apparently wasn't worthy. "When you're ready for a partner, I'll tell you," he said. "This is for your own good, you know. For the preservation of your ego. This isn't like the salsa, where you can just go out there unprepared and start shaking your ass like a whore. You go out there now, those women will eat you alive. Yes, they will." So walk I did, while El Tigre stood there and sipped his Johnny Walker—black label, no ice—and issued orders like: "Stand up straight! You have the posture of an eighty-year-old woman!" and, my personal favorite: "You have the virility of a fork!"

In my defense, this was nothing like normal walking. To walk like a proper tango dancer, I had to lean forward on the ball of my foot and take tiny, nibbling steps, dragging my heel along behind. "If anybody at the milonga ever sees the bottom of your heel, they'll think you're an *exhibicionista*, and no one will ever speak to you again," El Tigre warned. He didn't explain this bewildering assertion any further, but I did my best to comply. It was a supremely awkward way to move, though, like shuffling through mud with loafers on, and I kept losing my balance and staggering into the long wooden bar. Complicating matters further, El Tigre had ordered me to walk as if I was leading an imaginary tango partner—a brown-eyed,

Spanish beauty, I had (rather pitifully) decided—with my left arm flared out, holding her hand, and my right arm holding the small of her back. Most impossibly of all, he had ordered me to move while keeping strict time with the music. Given the anarchic syncopations of the tango, with its wailing violins and unconventional $3/4$ time, I never stood a chance.

All of this suggested that maybe I did need walking practice after all. But the horrible truth was that *everything* about the tango felt completely unnatural to me. I had always assumed that most dancing was supposed to be spontaneous; that you were supposed to listen to music, react to it, and move accordingly, each man to his own drummer. On the other extreme, there were dances like the waltz or the two-step that were regimented and set and maybe a bit overbearing, but at least they were straightforward. The tango was like a horrible hybrid, neither structured nor free-form, and it came accompanied by a bizarre set of rules and codes. Apart from the warning regarding the display of my heels, El Tigre had already imposed upon me a dire list of do's and don'ts that seemed to rival the Ten Commandments in scope and tone:

- Never look a woman straight in the eye unless you want to dance with her.
- If a woman enters the milonga unaccompanied, she is probably a prostitute.
- The first thirty seconds of any tango are spent chatting idly with your partner. Acceptable subjects include the weather, the crisis, and the poetic beauty of the song that just ended. Marital status, real names, and neighborhoods of origin are strictly off-limits.

- *Never* talk to a woman once those thirty seconds are over and the dancing has begun. ("You wouldn't talk to a woman during sex, would you?" El Tigre had asked. He said this with such intense disgust that I decided not to answer the question truthfully.)
- A woman must be led with the torso, not with the hands or hips.
- Dancing more than one *tanda*—a series of four or five songs—with a woman over the course of an evening doesn't necessarily mean anything. Dancing two *tandas* back-to-back with the same woman means with absolute certainty that you will be getting laid.
- Whoever you dance the last tango of the night with, you get to take home.

In theory, many of these rules could have been attributed to old-fashioned chauvinistic Latin behavior, but there seemed to be a glaring flaw in this hypothesis: most Argentine men simply did not conform to the old-school, Julio Iglesias, *¿quien es mas macho?* stereotype of unbuttoned black silk shirts with gold chains and lots of chest hair. In fact, Argentine men were far more likely to be wearing a pink Polo shirt with a navy wool sweater tied around their neck (they were apparently unaware that *Miami Vice* had been canceled fifteen years previously). They tended to be rather slight in build and mild, even gentle, in demeanor; there was nothing remotely intimidating about most Argentine men. For every El Tigre sipping straight-up bourbon, there were at least five other men at the milonga drinking fruity frozen cocktails that no red-blooded, self-respecting American male would be caught dead consuming in public.

Perhaps more substantially, there did seem to be a rather progressive, even European attitude toward women in Argentine society at-large: there were plenty of females in the workforce and, particularly, in the Congress, where they were assumed to be much less corrupt than their thieving male counterparts.

Still, none of this liberal attitude seemed to have permeated the world of the milonga, and as I walked in endless circles and inhaled the stale cigarette smoke and stink of spilled red wine, I suddenly wasn't at all sure that I wanted to be a part of it. I was no angel, but I had been raised by a self-respecting divorced working mother who would have surely ordered me back to Texas had she known who her only son's role models were at this exact moment. And if dancing is primarily about the interaction between a man and a woman, did I really want to immerse myself in a dance defined by a retrograde, apparently dysfunctional, relationship? Maybe the Argentines had this tango mentality embedded in their DNA, and foreigners like me were simply incapable of understanding. After all, I saw no other non-Argentines at the Confiteria Ideal. Maybe I had chosen the wrong dance. Indeed, maybe I had chosen the wrong country.

As if reading my mind, El Tigre stepped toward me and shook his head gravely. "You have the wrong attitude," he said. "Watch this."

Then, the most extraordinary thing happened, almost too perfect to be real: El Tigre turned his head to the side, facing the dance floor, and his gaze honed in on a table on the other extreme of the room. With a barely perceptible flick of his chin, a redhead rose from her chair, as if summoned by telepathy, and she started walking toward us. Her hips sashayed more dramatically as she drew closer, and a contagious smile spread across her face. I must have smiled myself as it dawned on me that El Tigre had just wordlessly asked a woman to dance from a distance of more than twenty yards.

El Tigre looked at me and recognized my expression of wonderment. "*El cabaceo*," he said with a sly smile.

I had no idea what this meant, but I resolved to learn it.

The redhead nodded at El Tigre, and then, to my immense surprise, her eyes settled on me. "*Buenas*," she said, giving a slight, oddly endearing curtsy. "I'm Mariela."

I thought I saw El Tigre roll his eyes.

"Let's go dance, dear," he rumbled. He took her by the arm and escorted her out to the hardwood floor.

El Tigre danced the dirtiest tango I had ever seen. It was impossible to imagine two bodies more closely conjoined, moving in such perfect harmony. He glided around the dance floor, executing exotic moves that seemed solely designed to bring his partner even closer to him, if such a thing were possible. His hips rubbed up against hers, grazing but not grinding, leaving just enough to the imagination to make his moves that much filthier. If all the other dancers on the floor were rated R, El Tigre was a straight-to-home-video XXX. "You may not like my style," he had warned me, "because it's very rough, very homegrown. I don't clean up the dance. I just dance it as it comes. I'm like a musician who doesn't read sheet music, who just improvises." Whatever his philosophy, I had to give the man due credit. Watching the two of them dance, the tango seemed erotic, extraordinarily seductive. And thus I remembered what I was doing here— The Godfather, with his aura of a life well spent, was who I wanted to be in forty years.. El Tigre was who I wanted to be *right now.*

The presence of Mariela certainly helped. She looked to be in her midtwenties, with a ballerina's lithe legs and thick red hair pulled into a tight bun. She was not conventionally beautiful, but *different*, somehow. She wore a long, backless red dress that looked like it was made of coarse, cheap material, maybe polyester. Most striking of all was the green tattoo stenciled on the back of her bare right shoulder. From the corner of the bar, I couldn't quite see what it was, but something about the tattoo struck me as exotic. She seemed completely given over to the pleasure of the dance—macho or not, dysfunctional or not, she didn't really seem to care. She wore that same postcoital smile that all the skilled female dancers seemed to have, and of course, her eyes were completely, gloriously shut. By the end of the first song, I realized I was staring at her.

After a full *tanda*, the two of them parted. He pecked her on the cheek, walked back over to the bar, downed a shot of whisky, and looked me straight in the eye.

"I'm not an animal, you know," he declared, looking like he was about to claw my eyes out. "I love women. I do. So, don't think for a moment that I'm some kind of fossil. I've written screenplays. I've traveled the world. I listen to Bach. I'm a modern man. And don't forget it."

El Tigre projected the distinct air of someone who hadn't given a damn about anything for twenty years, but I had definitely stirred something deep within him. He was speaking with passion and an unprecedented degree of sobriety. "I don't know precisely what '*politicamente correcto*' means," he continued, wagging his finger at me, "but I can guess. My advice is not to bring that kind of thinking to the tango. The woman is treated a certain way, yes. Does she decide how to dance? No. Is she at the mercy of the man? Yes.

"But I'm going to tell you something. All this *machismo*, all this showmanship, there's a secret." He leaned into my ear and hissed: "*The women like it! Yes, it's true!*

"And no, this isn't some kind of *capricho argentino*. I've been all over the world, my friend, and everywhere it's the same: *las francesas, las alemanas, las inglesas, las chinas, hasta las norte americanas están locas por el tango.* They know a man when they see one. This is the way it has always been. The tango is more than a century old, my friend. If you want to understand why it is this way, then maybe you should go read the history. Look at the gauchos, the caudillos, the immigrants, and the whores—the people who made the tango what it is. Maybe there you'll find the answer.

"But do you want my advice? Don't complicate things, son. Just learn to tango. And if you do it correctly, you'll feel the force of it. You'll be dancing one day with a woman, and then it will hit you like lightning. When that finally occurs," he concluded with an abrupt, roaring laugh, "then you'll be a prisoner of the tango. Nobody will be able to save you! And then we'll see what happens! *¡Si, señor!*"

He punctuated his monologue with yet another swig of whiskey and then collapsed into a chair by the bar.

By sundown, we had both become extremely drunk. Fights never seemed to last very long in Argentina; they slipped away, forgotten, into the cigarette smoke. El Tigre spent the rest of the night dancing, each *tanda* with a different woman. I went back to dutifully practicing my walking in the corner, the circles getting broader and dizzier with each drink. Every few minutes or so, from the other side of the room, I heard Mariela's throaty laugh.

Toward the end of the evening, El Tigre tapped me on the shoulder and nodded in her direction. Smiling drunkenly, he asked, in a low, hoarse voice:

"*¿Divina la chica, no?*"

Mariela sauntered past us, heading for the bar. Then, as if on cue, she turned her head, looked right at me, and winked.

Little did I suspect, the trap had already been set.

I CRAWLED OUT OF BED AT TWO THE NEXT AFTERNOON AND took my hangover to La Biela, the center of the universe for the sort of Argentines who loved to wear navy blazers with gold buttons. (President De la Rúa would have been a regular—if he had been able to venture outside without fear of lynching.) It was a place where old *anglo-argentinos* smugly leafed through the *Financial Times*, holding their newspapers high in the air like a status symbol, either oblivious to—or unbothered by—the fact that the edition in their hands was already three days old. Such were the limitations of life at the end of the world, even for the elite, and La Biela was unquestionably a bastion of the elite—maybe second, in the public imagination, only to the opera house, the Teatro Colón. The symbolism had not been lost on the urban guerrilla groups of the 1970s who had bombed La Biela with particular zeal; the most recent renovation seemed to have occurred around that time, and the decor, like the customers, seemed frozen in a not particularly desirable moment in time. The ancient TVs were tuned not to Crónica, but Todo Noticias, its marginally upscale competitor. Light wood paneling adorned the walls, which were decorated with photos of unsmiling, famous local Formula One drivers (Argentines had pioneered auto racing, I was repeatedly assured) and mirrors, of course, lots and lots of mirrors.

There was something despicable about the place—that was certain. But La Biela did have two major characteristics working in its favor. First, it had unquestionably the best café con leche in the city, a rich, chestnut-flavored blend of coffee with milk so thick it was as if they had the cow tied up back in the kitchen. The brew was served in delicate green ceramic cups by waiters instilled with a military precision that never failed to shock me. Service elsewhere in Buenos Aires was all about sighs, disdain, and attitude; like so much else, this seemed to have been meticulously copied from the French. At La Biela, the influence was decidedly German (not for nothing did the Argentine elite feel at home here). The waiters—attentive, handsome men with cropped haircuts wearing green bow ties and vests who cheerily goose-stepped over to your table at the merest twitch of your finger—were all business. The coffee even came accompanied by a tasty little chocolate in green La Biela wrapping.

Second, La Biela's sidewalk patio was an unparalleled vantage point for beholding the zoo of Buenos Aires. The Argentine author Silvina Bullrich described La Biela as perhaps the only place in such a vast city where "people *knew* they would meet each other." Because, for all the city's reputed civilization, La Biela really was in a class of its own in that you could sit outside and have a coffee in complete peace. Elsewhere, clouds of diesel smoke billowed from buses, or the sidewalks were just too narrow, or the pigeons, the goddamn pigeons, would climb all over your table and try to steal your croissants or scratch your eyes out. There were no such problems at La Biela; maybe they had doused the place with DDT—I didn't really care. Here, you could sit in the shade beneath a giant gomero, the great monstrous tree of the Southern Hemisphere, and read a newspaper or a book in blissful silence. Off on the horizon, through the sculptures and kiosks of the Plaza Francia, you could barely see the red cranes of the port, lingering in the distance like a rumor. And just around the corner, seemingly twenty-four hours a day, was an old man in a derby hat with a guitar who played tango—not just for the tourists, but for the locals as well. Indeed, La Biela was a place where milongueros came during the day. Not all of them, of course; El Tigre wouldn't have been caught dead there. But I once saw Robert Duvall at La Biela (in a newspaper interview, he called it one of his favorite places in the whole world) and even the most hardened milongueros conceded that he was one *yanqui* son of a bitch who knew how to tango.

There were no Hollywood stars out on the patio today— just an Argentine guy my age with a little tuft of facial hair under his lip and wearing the standard pink Polo shirt, who was blithely complaining to his girlfriend about the atrocious boredom of his latest world tour.

"I went to Chicago," he sighed, "but there was *nothing* there."

"What a shame," his girlfriend said, with seemingly sincere compassion. "What about New York?"

"More or less," he said with a heavy shrug.

Clouds were conspiring above, but for now the glare was impossibly bright, enough that I thought I could feel my retinas boiling. This was the famous southern sun—Argentines said the ozone hole made the UV rays stronger, which seemed plausible even if you factored in the local penchant for exaggeration. It seemed as if a bright fluorescent light was illuminating the top of the gomero, like a Christmas tree with a star on top. Its giant, pear-shaped leaves waved lazily in the wind, glittering green and white and blue, and the last violet flowers of the jacaranda trees were tumbling to the ground like confetti. On spring days like this, you could almost inhale Argentina's fertility—it was enough to make a man mad.

I had decided to obey El Tigre's instructions and buy a book on the history of the tango. I had done my homework and trolled the great bookshops of Avenida Corrientes—the ones that were still open, anyway—asking for the best, most comprehensive tome on the subject. I had been directed to the authoritatively named *El Tango*, written by a respected Argentine essayist and poet named Horacio Salas. But just half an hour into my reading on the fabulous La Biela terrace, I discovered to my dismay that neither Salas nor anybody else seemed to have the slightest clue where the tango had come from. Its origins were a near-total mystery; there were some hints, some theories, a few rumors here and there, but that was the extent of it. At least Salas had sense enough to be honest about this. The first sentence of his book—*the* definitive book on tango history—read: "When neither documents nor witnesses exist, the reconstruction of an event is always imaginary." Well, yes, that's one way of putting it.

Nobody could even agree on where the word "tango" had come from. According to Salas, there were at least twenty theories on the subject. Some of them were laughably bizarre—and yet, none of them could be thoroughly disproved. Some historians believed that "tango" was derived from "*tambo*," itself a corruption of the Spanish word *tambor*, or drum. Others noted that Tango was a place name in both Angola and Mali, which informed one of several theories centering on an African origin—despite the painfully obvious fact that there were almost no black people to be found in Argentina. Another theory held that, as early as the eighteenth century, there was already a couples' dance called the tango—in Mexico. And maybe the wildest theory of all came from a 1930s-era historian named Eduardo S. Castilla, who posited: "The word tango is Japanese. A city and a region in the Empire of the Rising Sun had that name. It is also the same name as one of the five popular festivals in that country. It is celebrated the fifth day of the fifth month of the year and is a symbolic date for children. In Cuba, there were many Japanese during the middle of the eighteenth century, and it was coincidentally in Cuba where tango was danced for the first time."

I slammed the book shut and wondered: were there any absolutes in this country? Just across the street, behind a Mercedes, a couple of street kids had dropped their pants and were urinating. One of the waiters walked over and shooed them away before anyone else among the clientele at La Biela noticed.

Just then, a little bit of rain was spit from the sky. Thunder rumbled dramatically, and people started to run inside, anticipating the typical big *pampero* thunderstorm. The same waiter stood there by the door, tray in hand, looking down his nose, as if running away would utterly violate his sense of dignity. "They're just a few drops. Ultimately, without consequence," he announced to everyone, and no one in particular.

Before long, it was just me and the waiters out on the patio. The sun was still shining intermittently through the clouds while a cool, moist wind gusted downward. I turned to the waiter, grinned, and asked: "Can I get a weather forecast for the next fifteen minutes?"

He indulged me with a thoughtful frown, stroking his moustache as he held up his finger to the wind. "I'll go call El Supremo," he said with a sly smile, "and see what he says. But I think he's going to send some more water."

The waiter disappeared inside and never came back.

Fifteen minutes later, like pieces on a chessboard, the thunderclouds had moved into position. The rain started coming down in sheets. Checkmate. I scurried inside and claimed a table by the window. Outside, several girls in their early twenties were laughing and running through the rain, seeking shelter under La Biela's green awnings, sliding around in their sandals on the slick sidewalk.

And that was when I finally decided: To hell with El Tigre. I was going to go tango with some real girls.

I HAD HEARD ABOUT LA ESTRELLA, A MILONGA THAT DREW a younger crowd and offered group lessons where, lo and behold, you could actually dance with members of the opposite sex. What kind of milonga catered to people in their twenties? I set out that Saturday night with visions of a sleek, steel-and-glass structure, maybe on the northern shores of the Río de la Plata out by the other hot nightclubs. Neon lights, house music between *tandas* of tango? Sure, why not? It would be perfect—all of the human warmth and sexual tension that the tango offered without any of the bullshit codes espoused by El Tigre and the rest of the old guard. I was rather surprised, then, when my taxi pulled up in front of a modest 1970s-era building with a sign outside that said "Centro Cultural Armenio." As I pulled open the glass double doors to go inside, I nearly collided with a group of small children in formal dresses and suits escorted by a mafia of white-haired, bearded old men in tuxedoes.

A little blonde girl looked up at me and smiled. "Hello, sir," she said excitedly in English. She pointed behind her, up the stairwell. "Are you here for the Armenian Argentine Chess Championship?"

I glanced upstairs and, for the briefest of moments, considered it. "No," I responded, feeling strangely disappointed. "I'm here for the tango."

"Chess, upstairs," her grandfather said with a thick, unfamiliar accent. "Tango, downstairs."

I thanked them, descended to the basement, paid a five-peso admission, and walked straight into Memphis, Tennessee, circa 1955.

> *Oh, what a crazy party all the gang's here, too*
> *The beat is really jumping like a kangaroo*
> *I'm full of cherry soda and potato chips*
> *But now I want to get a taste of your sweet lips*
> *So, dim, dim the lights!! Dim, dim the lights. . . .*

Here before me, in a dark, low-ceilinged, utterly claustro-phobic room, was a mob of Argentines doing a dance I vaguely recognized (again, from movies) as the jitterbug. Two by two, the crowd spun around in near-unison, like it was some kind of USO show or a choreographed dance num-ber in an Elvis Presley film. At the front of the room were a young man and woman, no older than twenty, dressed all in black, barking out dance instructions with the fervor of boot camp instructors: "Forward! Back! With your right foot! Now spin!"

I stood there, bewildered, as it fully dawned on me that I was watching two hundred people dance to Bill Haley and His Comets in the basement of an Armenian cultural center in the middle of South America.

A thick cloud of cigarette smoke hovered over the room like fog. The space itself was sparsely decorated—"retro min-imalist," the owner would proudly tell me—with little glit-tery cardboard stars and a disco ball suspended from the ceiling. The green plastic tables looked like they had been purchased secondhand, and they were draped with red and white tablecloths that were pockmarked with cigarette burns. Gold, white, blue, and orange stage lights were sus-pended in a row, casting a schizophrenic glow across the black tile dance floor.

"Half a turn! Another turn! Half a turn! Good! Half a turn!"

There was a little bar on an elevated platform near the en-trance. Someone had scrawled a list of drinks on a chalkboard:

Fernet Cola $4
Cuba Libre $4
Gin/Vodka Tonic $4

Daiquiri $5
Destornillador $5
Sex on the beach
*   (te empomo en la playa) $5*
Caipirinia $5

The bartender, a jolly-looking Italian, walked over. "What can I serve you?"

"Do you have beer?"

Over time, I would learn there is a particular face Argentines make when they feel a foreigner has completely underestimated their country. It could be described as a wounded grimace, anger mixed with pride and one hell of an inferiority complex. The bartender's expression, in this case, was intended to convey to me more or less the following: "Yes, you ignorant *yanqui* twit, we may be a distant South American country that most of your compatriots have never heard of, but believe it or not, we do have beer here. We have running water, too. Now go fuck yourself."

Too polite to actually say this, like most Argentines, the bartender simply responded under his breath, "Yes, we have beer," handed me a bottle of Quilmes from beneath the counter, and sulked away.

A Buddy Holly song ended, and with it, apparently, the jitterbug class.

The crowd here was solidly, almost breathtakingly middle-class. People had cell phones proudly clipped on their belts—status symbols, just as people had done five years before in the United States.

The DJ was now playing some Sinatra, apparently to bide time.

Suddenly, a voice: "Chino, the lights!"

The bartender took off running toward the far corner of the room.

Someone yelled, in heavily accented English, "*Run, Forrest, run!*"

The room went dark, and, with a mood shift worthy of a true manic depressive, the lights flashed back on, the disco ball started spinning, and—by this point, I can't honestly say I was surprised—loud and clear through the speakers came Technotronic's hyperactive 1989 dance club anthem "Pump Up the Jam."

A clean-cut middle-aged man in a black suit and a white headband sprinted to the middle of the room and started jumping around to the beat, like Rocky warming up for a title bout. "Welcome! Welcome to La Viruta!" he exclaimed. "Welcome! What a pleasure to see all of you!" He pulled a confused-looking girl out of the crowd and literally started humping her leg. "*¡No logro controlarme el miembro!*" he exclaimed—"I'm unable to control my member!" He laughed hysterically and the girl, with great effort, managed an obliging smile.

"Advanced class, upstairs with Angela and the fabulous Horacio Godoy!" he continued, still grinning like a maniac. "Intermediates, here in the middle of the room with Mecha and Carlos! Those who have practiced their *ochos* and *giros*, you're right here to the side! And those who have never taken a tango class in their lives, *los principiantes*: Welcome, friends! You're by the bar, with Mercedes and Mati!"

The clientele here was predominantly under forty, and there was certainly a fair share of young, gorgeous Argentine women. But as the crowd divided up, I noticed that the most attractive girls all seemed to be heading for the advanced classes upstairs. Beauty seemed to be directly proportional to skill level. I meekly shuffled over to join all my fellow uglies in the *clase de los principiantes.*

Approximately one in three of the men present had mullets—not just any mullets, but giant 1980s-style glam rocker mullets: curly in the back, with gel applied throughout. There were several older men on the prowl, including a few with horribly botched face-lifts who looked immutably surprised as they scanned the room for babes. That department was notably thin; there was nobody of real note, good or bad, except for an octogenarian lady in the back with a pearl necklace, a hangdog frown, and an enormous calcified hump on her back.

"You'll be dancing soon, so start looking now for the partner of your dreams!" declared the teacher, Mercedes, as the class gathered in a semicircle around her. She looked no older than twenty-five and had stunning blonde hair that tumbled down to her waist. Her gaze lingered on no one particular person for longer than two seconds at a time; there was nothing to see in this class, and she had no illusions to the contrary. Yet, she possessed an easy smile and would manage throughout the class to do an exceptionally good job of pretending that we weren't all completely hideous.

The class separated again, this time by sex, with the men facing the women in rows, while Mercedes had us practice what she called *el paso básico.* This was basically a series of seven steps—mostly forward for the men, mostly backward for the women—in the shape of a C, with a pause at the midpoint. Apparently, this pause was the moment in the sequence in which you could do all the funny business with the spinning and the hooks between the legs; but that would all come later. For now, we just practiced the paso itself, 1–2–3–4–5–6–7, over and over, for a good twenty minutes.

"Now, go!" Mercedes said with a bemused grin, taking obvious pleasure in ordering the mass tango deflowering of a crowd of thirty people. "Go and find yourselves a partner! But remember—if it's a complete disaster, we always change partners every two songs! So don't panic! And careful with those hands, ladies!"

This made everybody laugh.

I gazed toward the upper level by the entrance, where the advanced class was happily dancing away. There, the skirts were short, the backs were bare, and the steps were convoluted and seemingly impossible. That would all have to wait. But I was also shocked to see that all the girls my age were completely monopolized by men over sixty-five.

"Dance with me."

This was an order. I turned around and saw that it had been delivered by the hunchbacked old lady with the pearls, standing before me with her hands placed on her hips. Apparently my chronic grass-is-greener complex had distracted me enough to allow this silent eighty-year-old assassin to sneak up behind me when I wasn't looking. Everybody else in our class had already paired off. She looked up at me sternly, expectantly, from nearly a foot and a half below. I instantly knew that there would be no refusing her.

So my first tango would be with a grandma. Well, I thought, who would know? And at that instant, I had one of the first great revelations of my time in Argentina: I was 5,000 miles away from anybody I knew, and thus, really for the first time in my entire life, I had complete freedom to do anything I wanted without anybody ever finding out. I was accountable to absolutely no one. If I wanted to dance with this woman for the rest of the night, I could. If I wanted to take her back to my apartment and start a torrid May–December romance, so be it. What the hell.

I took a step closer, fanned out my left hand like I had seen El Tigre do a thousand times, and pulled Quasimodo toward me.

"*Listo?*" I asked.

She nodded with satisfaction. "*Vamos.*"

We lurched our way through the first few steps, 1–2–3–4. With each movement forward, my right hand grazed her hump. It was uneven, sharp like a jagged rock.

Mercedes walked by, inspected our form, and frowned. "You need to be closer together," she said. She put her hand flat on my back and pushed me toward my partner.

Grandma's breasts were now balancing on my belt.

"That's better," Mercedes said, and I thought I glimpsed a mischievous smile on her face as she walked away, leaving the two of us to fend for ourselves.

We took another few steps.

I looked down at my partner.

"You dance very well," she said with a smile.

"Thanks," I replied with a sigh. "So do you."

———

YOU HAVE TO PROMISE YOU WON'T DANCE WITH ANY women until I say you're ready."

"I promise."

"You have to promise that you'll practice walking for several hours a day."

"What?"

"Are you serious about this or not?"

"Okay, okay, fine."

It was the following Thursday night, and I was standing there at the Niño Bien, hat in hand, groveling before El Tigre, trying to get him to take me back under his wing. An entire junta of elderly men, all of them impeccably dressed in fine suits and with their hair slicked back with generous quantities of mousse, had gathered at El Tigre's table, like the board of directors for an absolutely fabulous corporation. I thought I recognized some of them as the exact same men who had so improbably monopolized the women at La Viruta a few nights before. Perhaps they were now engaged in negotiations to divvy up the coming Saturday night's catch in advance—"Okay, you can take the young *cordobésa* on the 2 A.M. to 4 A.M. shift." . . . "But he got the blonde last week!"—in between highballs and cigarettes. They regarded me out of the corners of their eyes, somewhat amused by the spectacle of an American a quarter of their age begging for forgiveness, but mostly focused on the real action on the dance floor.

El Tigre nodded with apparent satisfaction and made a broad sweep of the table with his giant hand. "Well, you can join us. This will be good for you, actually. Every single person at this table is a legend. This, Brian, is the *consejo de mayores*. Welcome."

The "Council of Elders"?

The group that first night included El Dandy, El Nene ("The Kid") Patterson, El Viejo Dani ("Old Danny"), El

Chino ("The Chinaman"), Hector El Griego ("Hector the Greek," who was actually Italian), El Chino #2, El Gil ("The Doofus"), Juan el Negro ("Juan the Black," who was not even remotely black), and a few other minor personalities. (Perplexingly, about one in five milongueros seemed to be nicknamed "The Chinaman," which could apparently be used to describe anyone with narrow eyes and a vaguely yellow complexion. No one seemed to realize this was almost certainly because they had South American Indian, rather than Chinese blood. Far better to be a *chino*, it seemed.) Everybody had a nickname but me, and everybody seemed to be over the age of sixty except the incongruous El Chino #2, who appeared to be my age or slightly older. They all smiled at me politely, without enthusiasm, as I sat down.

El Nene Patterson, dressed in a dark Armani suit and with an unruly shock of reddish hair on his head, leaned forward, put his hands on the table palms-down, and addressed me in a pitch-perfect Irish brogue that made my jaw drop.

"So, son, why do you want to learn the tango?"

I shrugged. "To meet people, I think."

"Good, good. Don't worry, son. We're going to get you laid." He said this in a businesslike tone that I found tremendously reassuring. Then he switched seamlessly into full-fledged porteño Spanish and raised his voice to the rest of the table. "Gentlemen, we need to teach this boy a few of the *códigos de la milonga*."

The waiter approached our table.

"What can I get you gentlemen tonight?"

El Nene peered at everyone over his glasses. He possessed a statesmanlike quality that granted him the authority to take care of the truly crucial business, such as ordering drinks. After a brief sweep to count the number of people at the table, he cocked his head. "The usual?"

Everyone growled their agreement.

"Nine strawberry daiquiris, please."

"With sugar?" the waiter asked.

"Of course."

"Wait—Brian, do you want a daiquiri?"

"Yeah, I'd like a daiquiri."

"*Diez daiquiris de frutilla, por favor.*"

The waiter made a solemn note of this and walked away.

The man named El Dandy leaned in, took stock of me, crinkled up his nose in disgust, and looked away. El Dandy was the most outlandishly dressed of the group, boasting a white terrycloth suit with a tangerine shirt that was monogrammed DJG. (That was the closest I would ever come to knowing his real name; like the others, he kept his identity outside the milonga fiercely secret.) He also carried a white cane—only for show—and he had a red, Fernando de la Rúa–style ascot tied around his neck. Yes, El Dandy was a dandy. But it was also rather obvious that the clothes didn't really fit him; oh, they were immaculately tailored, of course, but this was clearly a man who had lived a less than genteel life. El Dandy's hands were chapped and scarred and calloused, and the lines on his face were like canyons into which his kind blue eyes disappeared when he laughed or frowned. He seemed to have a certain old warhorse quality about him, as if he was immensely tired but no one ever allowed him to sleep. His right knee was jittering up and down, up and down, as he sat there scoping out the room. Even less impressed by the crowd, his gaze finally, hesitantly, settled back on me, and he smiled with apparently authentic sympathy.

"*Pero no sos una bestia,*" he began. "You're not a beast. If I was blond like you, I'd get all the ladies. The things I'd do. . . . So what are you doing here with a *manga de viejos* instead of out dancing with a beautiful woman?"

"I don't know," I replied, feeling oddly defensive. "Why aren't you guys at home with your wives?"

He chortled. "*El que baila no se casa.*"

He who dances does not marry, El Dandy had said grandly, like the phrase had come from the mouth of Confucius himself.

El Chino #1, a silent type, who I don't think I ever heard speak again, rumbled in agreement: "It's true! I married the tango!"

They all laughed.

Our strawberry daiquiris arrived. They came with a little wedge of fruit perched on the side of the glass and a tiny white, sugary cookie.

"Are you guys retired?" I asked.

This question raised scandalized hackles from everyone at the table. "No!" they all protested.

"We tour the world!" El Dandy declared. "We're *profesores.*"

"I see," I said. Tango teachers always seemed to prefer the label *profesor* to the somewhat less grand *maestro*. "Where have you guys taught?"

"Everywhere! Italy, Finland, Australia, Japan. . . . "

"Your country," El Nene chimed in.

". . . France, Britain, the Philippines."

"I've been to Kansas City!" El Gil offered, proudly.

"That's marvelous," I said, taking a long sip out of the pink straw. "I had no idea there was so much demand out there for the tango. But if you guys weren't traveling the world giving classes, what do you think you'd be doing?"

"I don't know," El Nene said with a sly grin, "but I don't think we'd be playing chess."

"Is there anywhere you've been where they dance particularly well?"

"Nowhere!" El Dandy waved his hand in disgust. "Outside of Argentina, it's impossible for people to *feel* the tango. In other countries, we can teach them the steps, but they'll never dance like an Argentine. They look like puppets, you know? They move perfectly but they don't have any heart. Because if you don't understand the lyrics, you will never dance well. And they have no passion! It's disgusting!"

"I don't agree with that," El Nene said with a frown, thoughtfully stirring his drink. Everyone leaned in; he was the only man at the table who commanded full attention when he spoke. "I would say there *are* many foreigners who dance well. The Italians seem to understand the tango—there's a cultural affinity there, I suppose—but the Japanese also are enormously talented, and the Russians. . . . "

"Those Russians dance like a motherfucker," El Gil agreed. "It's incredible!"

"The key is to *understand* the tango," El Nene concluded. "If you become a real student of the dance, you can learn to dance well."

I nodded, still a bit dubious. "Is there a place in the world where *everyone* dances badly?" I asked.

"Miami!" several of them declared in unison.

This was met with uproarious laughter from the whole table.

"It's true," El Nene admitted with a defeated shrug. The table began buzzing with everyone's best Miami tale of woe. "*That* I agree with. I've spent many nights in Miami, and I tell you, it's a waste of time. Maybe it's the influence of the salsa. They all want to shake their ass like they're back in Havana, not in the milongas of Buenos Aires. If I could solve that problem, I'd be a millionaire."

"I guess some people are just lost causes," I said.

My voice must have been dripping with pessimism, because El Nene leaned forward in his chair like a hawk and evaluated me from head to toe, looking distinctly concerned. "Again, I disagree," he intoned confidentially, switching back to a precise, soft-spoken English, so that others at the table would not understand. "Maybe you've just had the wrong teacher. El Tigre is a decent man and a brilliant milonguero— one of the best—but in my opinion that man is too talented to teach. He doesn't understand why his students can't just automatically dance like he does. It's why Maradona could never be a soccer coach, you understand? I bet we could turn you into a decent dancer," he mused. "I mean, you're not exactly trying to make Broadway, are you?"

"No," I laughed. "I just want to meet. . . . "

"To meet people," he finished. "Right. You don't have to be so diplomatic with me, son. These Argentine girls, they're difficult, but . . . my goodness, they *are* worth the trouble. We'll get it all arranged." He straightened his glasses and smiled at me. "And I take it you're not from Miami?"

"No," I replied. "I'm from Texas."

El Nene's eyes widened, and for a moment he seemed to have stopped breathing. "That's okay," he gasped, finally. "It's okay. We'll manage."

With a crescendo, a new song was starting.

"Why don't you go show me how you dance?"

"I wouldn't know where to start," I said.

El Nene took me literally. "Well, you start with a good *cabaceo*."

"Right. How is that done?"

He shook his head in disgust. "¡*La puta que lo parió!* El Tigre, what have you been teaching this kid? Look, this is very simple, much simpler than the tango itself." El Nene rested his arm on my shoulder and leaned in confidentially. "You see that blonde over there?" He pointed to a non-Argentine-looking woman in her twenties sitting at a table by herself across the room. "You're going to ask her to dance."

"Do as I say now," he instructed with a whisper. "What you do first is you look around the room. Casually, at no one in particular. Good. Then, you allow your eyes to meet hers. She's not looking at you? It's okay, watch her until she looks at you. Keep watching. But not like a rapist! Good. Just relax. *Tranquilo.* Now . . . no, too long, now you have to look away . . . you should never hold her gaze for longer than three seconds. That's the rule. Now look back, and when she looks at you, just give her a little nod. Ready?"

The blonde looked over at me. Her eyes brightened and she started to stand up.

Ecstatic, I rose from my seat to go join her.

"No! No! God, no!" El Nene hissed. "You're not ready yet!"

I collapsed back into my chair, panicked. On the other side of the room, the blonde, confused, sunk back into hers also.

Everybody at the table was trembling with laughter.

"Come on! I'm joking! Go, go!" El Nene yelled, pushing me up onto my feet. "Go dance with the girl!"

As I started to get up again, I glanced over at El Tigre, who had been watching this whole sequence out of the corner of his eye with pronounced disinterest. I felt like a baton that had just been ceremoniously passed from one sprinter to another. He nodded his approval and gave me a laconic wink. I guess I was ready to dance with girls now. I crossed the room, took the blonde by the hand, and off we went.

W HEN I WAS SINGLE, I USED TO GO TO THE MILONGAS," Mónica was saying, "and the first thing I would say to each of my partners was: 'Don't fall in love with me, milonguero. Because you're going to lose the war.'" She laughed and threw her hands up in defeat. "That didn't stop them, of course. The milonguero lies. He cheats. He tries to touch your ass, touch your breasts. Like there was some kind of affinity there! Please! They plot among themselves, trying to seduce you. They tell each other: 'You didn't see me today.' Because most of these men are married. . . . "

"You make us sound like perverts," Carlos protested.

"No, no, not you, *querido!*" she cooed, slapping him playfully on the cheek. "That's why I took you home!"

We were at *La Cantina a los Amigos*, an Italo-Argentine restaurant in Old Palermo, celebrating two entirely unlikely developments: my apparent initiation into the world of the tango, for which Carlos and Mónica felt wholly responsible, and the signing of a contract for my first job, which was a direct consequence of Argentina's misfortune. The deepening economic crisis was creating more demand for news about Argentina on Wall Street and elsewhere, so the Reuters news agency had made me an offer to work as a financial reporter. I felt a bit guilty upon realizing that, from this moment on, the worse things got for Argentina, the better they would get for me professionally. Still, it was hard not to love the country on a night like this. Strands of garlic hung from the walls along with photos of professional boxers, tango dancers, Sinatra, Evita, Maradona, and the Pope (it was hard to imagine a collection of personalities that more distinctly reflected the porteño character; the only thing missing was a Marilyn Monroe poster). The paper tablecloths were rustling in the cool breeze, and the waiters were greeting every customer who came through the wooden double doors with a big kiss on the cheek. A kid in a Batman costume was running around the restaurant chopping the customers with his sword.

I figured that if there was one woman in Argentina who could have gone toe-to-toe with the men at the milonga, Mónica would have been her. She was glamorous and raven-haired, a self-made woman who had reinvented herself following a nasty divorce (is there any other kind?) as an immensely successful computer specialist and software writer. The daughter of an Argentine soldier, she gave classes on how to use Windows at the Circulo Militar, an astonishing old mansion on the Plaza San Martin that had been converted into the officers' club for the armed forces. In other words, Mónica spent most of her working hours trying to charm and simultaneously fend off lecherous old men, which was the closest approximation possible to a daytime milonga. I imagine they all must have been completely in love with her—she was in her midforties, refined, and possessed of a quiet, somewhat weary confidence that seemed newly won; I would bet this all made her much more attractive now than she had been two decades earlier. She also may have been the only person I knew who still made smoking look glamorous.

"You say what you feel, but the milonguero escapes," she continued. "He has his old codes, and he doesn't know any other kind of life."

"From the woman's perspective," I ventured, "it doesn't sound very attractive."

Here, Mónica sighed and took a long sip of wine. "This is hard to explain. . . . "

"She likes the abuse!" Carlos declared, laughing.

"¡Vos, callá!" she thundered. Then she laughed, almost giggled, and pushed him playfully on the shoulder. "No, I'm not a masochist. The truth is that the milonguero, while he can be disgusting and *machista* and tactile and false and a liar. . . . " "You really should be writing tourist brochures for Argentina," Carlos chimed in. ". . . These milongueros are like artifacts from a very different time," she said, very serious now. "They appeal to something very basic inside of all of us, something natural and—well, I don't know if it's positive, but it's natural, yes. I believe in women's rights, of course, but I also won't deny that on a fundamental level, men need to be men, and women need to be women. There are roles there. I'm sorry, but it's true. I had a friend who would accompany me, and do you know what she said to me each night? She said, '*Mónica, quiero que me abracen un poquito*—Mónica, I just want to be held a little bit.' And, yes, most of these men are trash, but there are a few true gentle-men among them, men who know how to dance correctly, and know how to really treat a lady. Those men are the *real* milongueros."

"Like The Godfather?" I asked.

"Who?"

"He means the man he met that first night with us at the Niño Bien," Carlos explained. "The man who everyone greets when they enter the room."

"Who?" she asked, still puzzled.

"You know," Carlos said, and then he uttered The Godfa-ther's real name.

"Oh." Mónica suddenly looked like she had seen a ghost. "No," she said softly, as if afraid someone would overhear her, "I don't quite mean *him*. But there are some real *caballeros* in the group. You just have to look."

Our pasta arrived. The 29th of every month in Argentina is traditionally known as *el dia del ñoqui*, a reference to a cheap meal of gnocchi pasta that everybody could afford at the end of the monthly pay cycle. The word "*ñoqui*" is also used to describe the hundreds of thousands of people (no-body knew for sure how many there were) on the govern-ment payrolls who receive a salary for no work—they appear in the office only on the 29th, to collect their checks.

"I met this other guy," I continued. "They call him El Nene Patterson. . . . "

"You know Patterson?" Mónica asked, her eyes bright.

"Yes, he gave me some advice. He taught me the *cabaceo*."

"*¿En serio?*"

"*En serio.*"

"*Que maravilla!*" Mónica declared, as bedazzled as a teenage groupie. "Now *that* is a real man!"

Carlos swiveled his head around, looking somewhat hurt.

"How do you know all these people?" I asked.

Mónica smiled. "That's the most fundamental truth about the milonga," she said. "Everybody knows everybody, even if they pretend they don't. Don't ever forget that."

The waiter brought us another sweating bottle of Quilmes beer and plopped it into the bucket of ice next to our table with a loud splash.

"Did you have any success with your investigation of the history of the tango?" Mónica asked, sprinkling cheese on her *ñoquis.* "How did that go?"

"A total failure," I said, laughing.

A mischievous glint crossed Mónica's eyes. "You should ask Patterson about that," she said. "I recall him and his group being experts on the subject."

"What are you trying to do to him?" Carlos gasped, theatrically smacking his hand on top of his bald spot.

She shushed him playfully, raised her glass of beer, and proposed a toast. "To the tango," she declared with a laugh. "Wherever the hell it came from!"

S O TELL ME," I SAID, EASING INTO MY CHAIR, "WHO INVENTED the tango?"

"*¡Que lo parió!*" one of the men exclaimed, pounding the table. Everyone's espresso sloshed onto the tablecloth. "Who put you up to asking that?"

"Too much, too much," El Chino #1 muttered, shaking his head. He rose to his feet, ruefully crossed himself, kissed the top of his fist, and stomped away toward the parquet dance floor, mumbling under his breath, "*Que barbaridad.*"

Those left at the table, the other delegates of the Council of Elders, continued to stare at me as though I'd just called their mother a whore.

I sat there, looking appropriately traumatized, I'm sure. After a silent eternity, El Nene Patterson took a sip of beer and put a reassuring arm around my shoulder. He looked over his eyeglasses at me with a grim but sympathetic smile.

"You've walked into a hundred-year-old war here," he explained.

"I see, but. . . . "

"And I will *choose* to assume that you have no idea what you've done."

"That's correct," I stammered. "But why did. . . . "

"I think everyone can relax," El Nene declared, interrupting me again, leveling his gaze slowly around the table, "and perhaps apologize to our guest, who was unaware of his sin, and we can all pretend this episode never happened."

The other old men at the table cast their eyes downward. A few of them seemed to be barely suppressing smiles, though I couldn't quite be sure.

"Very good," Nene said gravely. He was serious as a mortician. "It's over. Who wants more coffee?"

The noisy clutter of the tango soon made us forget. The man who had bitterly left our table a mere minute before, El Chino #1, was now gliding along the dance floor with a brunette who was at least six inches taller and forty years younger than he was. He rested his cheek blissfully on her breast, his eyes nearly closed, as they floated around the room.

"Good Lord," I muttered, pointing. "Can he *do* that?"

"Yes," Patterson said with a wry grin, "he certainly can."

We traded smirks and toasted the old lecher with our beer. A waitress brought us some midnight espressos. Everything was grand.

"It was the gauchos."

I swiveled around and saw El Dandy, the weary old dilettante with the white cane. He was grinning like he had just swallowed a canary.

"Pardon me?" I asked, sensing that Pandora's Box had just been opened.

"The gauchos invented the tango," El Dandy replied. "It can be proven."

Everyone else at the table erupted in a series of groans.

"This bullshit again?" someone shrieked.

"It's not bullshit," El Dandy protested, his frail voice cracking with emotion. "Any milonguero who knows anything can see that *el tango es de los gauchos.*"

El Nene sighed, threw up his hands in surrender, and started shaking with laughter. "You illustrious old farts can debate this again for the zillionth time, if that's what you really want," he declared, standing up from his chair, still laughing, "but I'm going to go lose myself in the embrace of a beautiful woman. *Con permiso.*"

El Dandy edged his chair closer to mine. The laughter lines around his face had disappeared. "Where are you from, son?"

"Texas."

"Spectacular!" he said. His voice still trembled with anger. "You will understand, then. Because, you see, the cowboys of

Texas were very similar to the gauchos in Argentina. They were cousins, you could say. Both of the races lived on horses, they lived by the knife, they never settled with just one woman. And they each had their music. The cowboys invented *la música country*, and the gauchos invented the tango.

"The tango reflected realities in the gaucho's everyday life," he continued. "You can still see the gaucho's life in the tango. The music was contemplative, melancholy. And who could blame him? Surrounded by a thousand kilometers of nothing on each side, of course the gaucho was going to get a bit philosophical!" He laughed. "It was the music of the frontier, of the empty space. And you can see the gaucho's life in the dance, too. Whether it was the movement of a horse," he said, standing up from the table, taking a few rapid, exaggerated steps back and forth, "or a knife fight."

He lunged forward, making a thrusting motion that, in the shadows, did *slightly* resemble a tango step. Perhaps.

"The tango was about the gaucho's very existence. It was their religion. The gaucho didn't think about it. That's just how he was.

"But then," El Dandy went on, his upper lip stiffening with operatic rage, "Argentina began to change. For the worse, if you ask me. The immigrants started coming from Europe. The *campo*, the countryside, was closed with fences. The gaucho moved to the city, and he saw that the immigrant had skills. The gaucho started wondering what skills he had, what he could possibly give to society. So the gauchos taught the immigrants how to dance the tango. In exchange these Europeans taught them skills like tailoring, carpentry, whatever they knew from Naples or Seville.

"Of course, I think the immigrants ended up winning in that equation. Because the gauchos had this marvelous tradition—what a lovely race!—where they were able to capture women. They sang to them, they told them 'I love you,' they charmed all the beautiful girls with the tango. And that's far more important than being able to stitch up a suit, if you ask me.

"But once that knowledge was passed on, the gaucho was left with nothing. It was as if he had killed his own cow. Therefore," El Dandy concluded, a melancholy smile on his face, "after he taught the tango to the immigrant, that was the moment in history that the gaucho disappeared from Argentina forever."

I sat in stunned silence.

"Utter bullshit," someone at the table finally growled.

"He's lost his mind."

"Do you see any gauchos around here?"

"Why would. . . . "

"You can all go to hell," El Dandy countered, his voice measured and quiet. "I know what the *argentino autentico* is. Anyone who disagrees is a *gil* and I will take you outside and I will kick your ass, I swear by the Virgin Mary, if you say otherwise. At the very least," he said, turning to me with a wink, "let's allow the young Texan to search for the answers himself."

AT FIRST GLANCE, IT IS IMPOSSIBLE TO IMAGINE THAT BUENOS Aires could ever have been a cowboy town. Could Carlos

Gardel *really* have had anything in common with Hank Williams? In the cosmopolitan city that I know, there are no rodeos. Nobody wears cowboy hats to the Teatro Colón. Wearing boots is a sure way to get thrown out of a nightclub. And there certainly are no gauchos walking around town, save for a few on Calle Florida to charm the tourists.

In fact, the modern-day residents of Buenos Aires were remarkable for just how thoroughly they turned their backs on Mother Nature. To be fair, they live in a city that is hemmed in on all sides, not by jungle or desert but something far more formidable—emptiness. To the south and west, once you pass the endless suburbs on the old British-built railroad lines, there sit hundreds of miles of featureless Pampa, plains unsuitable for hiking or most other worthy outdoor pursuits. On the other side of the city is a muddy, churning, atrociously polluted river that measures fifty miles from shore to shore and is utterly useless for recreation. My first boss, a freckly Brit, had taken windsurfing lessons on the Río de la Plata and was rewarded with a near-fatal ear infection. Within Buenos Aires, there is a modest supply of parks and gardens, but they are overwhelmingly concentrated on the northern side of the city by the river, in the richer neighborhoods like Palermo, Belgrano, and Nuñez. For most of the city's other residents, particularly the poorer ones, it is possible to live an entire lifetime without seeing an open space bigger than a plaza.

Thus, Buenos Aires is a virtual concrete island unto itself, more Manhattan than Fort Worth. On weekends, porteños of all ages go to bed at 4 A.M., wake up at noon, and spend their Sunday afternoons either in cafés or at grandma's house eating ravioli. It isn't just that they never venture outside—they don't even seem to be *aware* of the concept. After all, you can't miss something you have never experienced. Whole lives are spent indoors, out of the sun. Even on "outdoor adventure" trips to Patagonia, one of the world's last truly wide open spaces, I saw how tourists from Buenos Aires would nervously seek out their own kind, congregating in groups of fifty to chain-smoke together by the side of a glacier and gossip about the latest political scandal. "Where's the nearest café?" they would ask, panicked like fish out of water. But they couldn't help it, the poor things; the porteños are a species raised in captivity.

How odd, then, that just a century before, Argentina had been home to one of the most wild and pure forms of boorish masculinity the world has ever seen. At around the same time the tango was emerging in its modern form—the 1860s, more or less—it was true that gauchos were still roaming the Pampa with reckless, gleeful abandon. Most of them ate nothing but steak, and the ground outside their cottages was usually covered with bones and the carcasses of cattle, producing an awful stench. They almost never bathed; instead, when it rained, gauchos were known to strip and then stuff their clothes under their horses' saddles to keep them dry, all while continuing to gallop along, now naked as the day they were born, at unthinkable speeds. They professed no interest in money and immediately and incontinently spent what little they had on wine, gin, and horses. The gaucho seldom cut his own beard and hair (though the mane of his horse was always assiduously trimmed). They did not marry, they did not read, and they usually slept under the stars on little more than a cowhide thrown across the Pampa grass. It was as if someone had put men in an environment with no rules, no women, and no responsibilities on a vast range with an infinite supply of meat and horses.

In other words, the gauchos had enormous fun. As Western travelers came in contact with them, the gauchos earned near-mythical status as thieves, gamblers, murderers, and mercenaries. Visitors with literary airs infallibly described them as centaurs—more than a few swearing that the gauchos were so wedded to their horses that they didn't even know how to walk. The air of mystery was heightened by the fact that no one really knew the gauchos' real origins; they were the illegitimate sons of Spanish conquistadores (who first brought the horse to the Americas) and the sparsely populated Indian tribes of the Pampa. Being nomads, though, it was impossible to know for sure—it's not like they were keeping family trees. In fact, being a gaucho was really more a question of lifestyle than ethnic identity; there was briefly a rather famous enclave of Jewish gauchos in Entre Ríos, near the border with Uruguay.

Their lifestyle was so attractive that in 1807, when British troops briefly invaded Buenos Aires as a strange and unexpected repercussion of the Napoleonic wars, the lure of the gaucho may have inadvertently changed the course of Argentine history. During the ensuing occupation, 170 British soldiers—a healthy percentage of the overall force—deserted their unit and went native, apparently finding the gauchos' lifestyle preferable to their own. After four months of attrition, the remaining force became small enough to be half-heartedly chased out by the porteños, who poured tar on the British troops as they retreated to their boats. Years later, the British commander still seemed shocked by the cause of his defeat: "The more the soldiers became acquainted with the plenty the Country affords and the easy means of acquiring it, the greater the evil," he glumly noted. Indeed, it is possible that but for the free-wheeling gauchos, Argentina might have become part of the British Empire.

G. Whitfield Ray, an American adventurer and rather puritanical part-time missionary who traveled widely across the continent and was described by one admirer as "the Livingstone of South America," spent time with the gauchos and, while a bit wary of them, he fully appreciated their appeal:

> The forward march of the outer world concerns him not. Indeed he imagines that his native prairie stretches away to the end of the world. . . . He is subjected to no kind of restraint, as he sees nothing but lakes, rivers, and deserts, with now and then naked straggling men pursuing wild beasts and bulls. He becomes habituated to the same sort of life, and to independence: he knows neither rule nor measure in any thing; he dislikes the society of persons whom he does not know, and to the love of country, modesty, decency, and the conveniences of life, he is an utter stranger. . . . Living the wild, free life of the Indian, and retaining the language of Spain; the finest horsemen of the world, and perhaps the worst assassin; the most open-handed and hospitable, yet the accomplished purloiner of his neighbor's cattle . . . spending his whole wealth in heavy gold or silver bell-shaped stirrups, bridle, or spurs . . . and leaving his home destitute of the veriest necessities of life—such is the Gaucho.

Fancying himself quite the Indiana Jones, Ray hired gauchos to serve as his guides on a journey across the Pampa. It seems, however, that Ray didn't quite realize what he was getting himself into. The missionary watched in abject horror as his traveling companions cleaned their mouths with their knives and used their horsetails to clean, ahem, their unmentionable parts. Ray positively squirmed when he noticed how some gauchos kept a stash of raw beef between their saddles and their horses' backs, a kind of nineteenth-century predecessor to jerky, ripping off chunks of flesh whenever they felt hungry. "We should imagine that in the hot months, after a hard day's ride, it can require but little cooking," he noted. Ray was obviously charmed in many ways by the gauchos, but it is also quite clear that the man was sleeping with one eye open. "If you please him, he will present you with his best horse, waving away your thanks. If you displease him, his long knife will just as readily find its way to your heart."

The gaucho uniform, such as it existed, was an appropriately colorful mix of cowboy and Indian. The gaucho wore a shirt and a slouch hat, but the similarities to European dress ended there. He usually wore tall boots that were made from one seamless piece of hide—usually the hind legs of a horse. The bend of the horse's leg served as the boot's heel, and the toes protruded from the front (covered shoes were not desirable because the gaucho never put more than his big toe in the stirrup). He carried trinkets on his breast, and on bullets he often scratched the sign of a cross. If the gaucho was young and single, he also tied on an owl's skin to ensure himself luck with the ladies and a safe arrival. Around his waist was a long, colored belt with tasseled ends that hung down to his boots, and over that, a broad belt of animal skin, cinched at the front with silver and adorned all around with gold or silver coins. Within that belt, the gaucho sheathed his infamous knife, the same long blade that apparently kept Ray awake at night.

"Of knives he possesses more than enough, and heavy, long, sharp-pointed ones they are," Ray noted, sounding more and more like a man who hadn't slept for several days. The gaucho used the knife to dip each bite of beef in a fire's ashes, instead of using salt. "When his hunger is appeased the knife goes, not to the kitchen, but to his belt. With that weapon he kills a sheep, cuts off the head of a serpent, sticks his horse when in anger and, alas, as I have said, sometimes stabs his fellow-man."

Yet, for all his squeamishness, Ray would certainly have needed their help. Today, the Pampa seems dull—nothing but fields of wheat and soy and the occasional *estancia*—and in the modern era of highways and grain silos, it is supremely benign. Not so long ago, however, the Pampa was still an untamed wasteland that elicited dread in those who were obligated to cross it. The region was variously described as "an ocean of land" and a "kingdom of silence," complete with a litany of hazards that read like something out of the Book of Revelation: mosquitoes, tarantulas, snakes, and roaming packs of ravenous wild dogs. Locusts were so common that Argentine farmers, obviously driven to the brink of insanity, seriously considered building a giant zinc fence in the northeast to keep the bugs out. Trains would become stuck on railway lines, their wheels spinning in a pool of dead locusts. Meanwhile, thunderstorms swept into the Pampa from the Andes with frightening speed, the deluge sweeping away entire caravans of would-be settlers. When there was no flood, there was drought. Sometimes you had both: dust storms mixed with rain storms, producing a torrent of wet mud that coated houses, fences, and all else in a grimy goo. The only food to be found was an occasional dove, or perhaps a giant turtle hauled out of a flooded ditch by the side of the road. The foreboding highways were littered with abandoned wagons and bleaching bones.

"It is more like going to sea than traveling by rail," wrote Burton Holmes. "The sea itself could not afford so much of sameness, so sad, unbroken a monotony. The towns seem like small groups of shipwrecked houses that have drifted over league after league of level waveless land to moor themselves near the railway line."

Yet, the gauchos were most at home in this environment, and their skills were put to good—if ultimately self-destructive—use by men much less scrupulous than G. Whitfield Ray. During the civil war that raged in Argentina for much of the nineteenth century, as the government in Buenos Aires sought to exert centralized authority over the vast, untamed interior, gauchos were hired as armies of galloping cavalry. The gaucho armies were fast-moving, greatly skilled at employing a knife, and utterly lacking in morals; they must have been absolutely terrifying opponents. The gauchos were again used as mercenaries in the so-called Desert Campaign to track down and exterminate the last roaming tribes of Argentine Indians—people with whom the gauchos shared both ancestry and a lifestyle. When Charles Darwin visited Argentina, he was stunned by the gauchos' ability to pursue Indians for hundreds of miles at a time, over the Andes and even into Chile to kill them off. "What other troops in the world are so independent?" Darwin wrote. "With the sun for their guide, mares' flesh for food, their saddle-cloths for beds—as long as there is a little water, these men would penetrate to the land's end."

So: how could a seemingly morose dance like the tango have originated with such a happy, carefree people? On the surface, one appears to have nothing to do with the other. Indeed, the gaucho would seem to be the antithesis of the modern porteño. But whatever contribution the gauchos made to the music or the dance would in fact have come much later. For the tango was not the story of the gauchos' heyday, but that of their inevitable demise.

ONE NIGHT, EL NENE TOOK ME ASIDE IN CONFIDENCE. "IF EL Dandy hears me tell you this, he'll kill me," he whispered. "That crazy motherfucker keeps a switchblade in his left sock. *No te estoy jodiendo*—I am not kidding you. Tell me—is he looking at us now?"

On the other side of the room, El Dandy had his hands on a widow's ass.

I shook my head no.

"Good. Well, I'm here to tell you that El Dandy is right, but only *a medias*. I know that there are no gauchos anymore," El Nene said, peering at me over his glasses. "The point is: you have to realize what Argentina is made of. The gauchos are the people who gave us our identity. Whether there are still men walking down Avenida Corrientes wearing *bombachas* is irrelevant. Think about what the Puritans meant to the United States; are there still men in black hoods walking around New York? No! This was a group of, what, two hundred people who came over in the seventeenth century! But the Puritan ideal is still a fundamental part of who you Americans are. I mean that with all respect. You have the greatest country in the world; a little dull, maybe, but. . . . Look at the founding fathers of the United States—George Washington, Thomas Jefferson, those gentlemen. Why are you still so obsessed with obeying some document they wrote two centuries ago? Why?" He laughed. "As I understand it, your Supreme Court is entirely devoted to interpreting that Constitution, trying to figure out what those old guys wrote over the course of five minutes. And I think that's marvelous, I really do.

"So, with that in mind, take a look at our role models," he continued. "It's a couple of gauchos who were running around, cutting each others' throats, leaving their women, declaring war on everybody. So Dandy's right in one sense; these *were* the people who invented the tango, and who invented Argentina, but *this is nothing to be proud of!* Look at this place! These people were the foundation that everything else was poured on top of. It was the anarchy of the Pampa, where there was never a shortage of anything. There were no rules; maybe that's why we've had five thousand different constitutions." He threw up his hands and laughed. "And you wonder why we're so fucked up."

SUNDERLAND HAD A REPUTATION FOR BEING THE "PUREST" milonga, the place of choice for no-frills tango. El Nene despised it, thinking it unsophisticated; El Dandy believed it was the only venue truly worth his while. Whatever its merits, Sunderland was nothing more than an old basketball gymnasium located behind a social club. There were only four lights in the gym—blaring bright white stadium lights, two mounted on each side of the court. The only windows were small ventilation holes forty feet above the court, with metal bars across them. Basketball hoops hung from the ceiling, and exposed air-conditioning tubing ran along the wall. On the walls were ads for a bakery, the lottery, a glassmaker, sport shoes, a mechanic, a bookie, and a place called "Bubbles," offering home delivery, day care, baths, haircuts, and training—for dogs.

I straggled in to Sunderland one Saturday night, exhausted from an impromptu soccer match that afternoon with some of my new Argentine friends from outside the milonga. I had never played a minute of soccer prior to moving to Buenos Aires, but I had apparently entered an era of unrestrained experimentation. Now it was 1 A.M., the night was just beginning, and I was wondering why the hell everything in Buenos Aires always started so late.

El Dandy bounded over to my table, his eyes open so wide and his eyebrows arched so high that it was if he had just finished having a face-lift in the back room (this being Argentina, it was not out of the realm of possibility). He practically hopped with each word. "You look tired! Why are you so tired? It's too early to be so tired!" he blurted. "Come with me. I know how to wake you up."

Within ten seconds, I was shaking hands with the DJ. El Dandy introduced me as "Caruso"—the Council had decided that I needed a proper nickname, and Brian Caruso had been a child actor during the 1990s. El Dandy assured me that the DJ would take care of all my needs.

The DJ was grossly obese. He grunted hello and, by way of introduction, asked: "Do you know why this country is so messed up?"

I shook my head.

"*Porque todos somos re mil hijos de puta,*" he replied. "We're all real motherfucking bastards."

He laughed like Jabba the Hutt.

Then, his eyes shifted about, and he got down to business.

"What are you looking to buy?" he asked.

"I'm not sure," I answered, truthfully.

He pointed to a large stack of tango CDs. "All the great artists, all the great tango composers, right here," he was saying. "They can be yours. Good price."

"How much?" I asked.

"Five pesos."

For the moment, this was still equivalent to five dollars. "That's cheap," I replied.

"They're pirated."

"Is that fair?"

He looked at me like I was an alien. "Ah, well," the DJ said with a dismissive wave of his hand, "they're all dead anyway."

I considered this: not a bad point. I reached into my wallet and started to hand him a twenty-dollar bill.

"Sorry," he said, "*pesos argentinos* only."

I still had my hand in my wallet when I looked up and was startled to see The Godfather. I hadn't spoken to him since that first night at the Niño Bien. He had lipstick on his cheeks from greeting the crowd, and the same air of accomplishment and prestige that had drawn me to the tango in the first place.

"Buying something?" he asked, his eyebrow arched.

"Just a few CDs," I explained defensively, as if I had just been caught with porn. "They wouldn't be getting royalties anyway."

The Godfather nodded, disinterested. "Just some CDs?" he repeated.

I looked over at the DJ, who suddenly had an odd grin on his face.

"Yes," I replied, not yet understanding what this conversation was about. "Just CDs. Is there anything else to buy?"

"Are you sure you wouldn't like to buy anything more *interesting*?"

I looked at The Godfather, then back at the DJ.

The DJ tapped the side of his nose with his index finger.

They stared at me expectantly, like vultures.

Oh. . . .

"Yes, I think, just some CDs," I said. "Thanks, gentlemen."

WHEN I SAW HER A SECOND TIME, I FINALLY UNDERSTOOD the significance of her tattoo.

She was leaning over the bar at the Niño Bien in that same blood-red strapless dress, laughing heartily at something the bartender had said. I realized that the tattoo itself was not particularly remarkable—it was the fact she had one at all. Most Argentine women obsessively avoided such displays; they danced the same way, talked the same way, wore their hair the same way; usually, it should be conceded, to great effect. Nose rings, pink hair, and tattoos were positively unthinkable. But then here was this woman at the bar, drinking without shame, brandishing a tattoo of a scorpion, of all the unapologetically unsubtle things in the world. Her deep laugh echoed off the walls of the grand salon. This, I now realized, was not your typical *chica* porteña.

God bless the tango, I remember thinking. I actually have a legitimate excuse to invite this woman to dance.

I resolved to do it the right way. I would try out my *cabaceo*. As casually as I could, I strolled over to the opposite end of the bar and slowly allowed my gaze to settle on her. She continued to flirt with the bartender, looking everywhere but at me. I didn't stare at her, of course—I did as I had been told, holding my gaze for three seconds and then looking away, waiting a reasonable amount of time, and then starting the cycle over again.

She ordered a drink. She kissed someone hello on the cheek. Soon, I was just staring at her unabashedly. Then, just at the very moment I was starting to feel like a crazy sex offender, we made eye contact. A barely perceptible nod of my head and. . . .

She smiled. Eureka. She set her drink on the bar, winked enigmatically at the bartender, and turned my way.

"*¿Bailamos?*" she asked good-naturedly.

I grinned, so pleased with myself, and the tango, that I might explode. "*Bailamos.*"

I took her hand and dragged her, practically sprinting, over to the dance floor. The music struck up, I pulled her as close to me as I possibly could, and off we went.

It was like taking the wheel of a Mercedes-Benz. I was stunned by the ease, the smoothness of dancing with her. She seemed to respond to my every move with perfect, effortless precision. At the slightest shift in my shoulders, she would turn. A bit of pressure on her back, and she'd answer with a *giro*. Indeed, a few times she seemed to anticipate my lead before even I knew where I was going. Our bodies lined up with total symmetry; her waist at the same level as mine, her chest resting comfortably on my sternum. All my usual nervousness vanished. I started taking confident, sweeping steps, practically flying around the dance floor. Was I suddenly this good?

Well, no. In short order, I became so carried away that I started inventing steps. Through sheer skill, she managed to stick with me for a while, but soon, after a particularly ill-advised *ocho*, I found myself trapped. I froze, flat-footed, both feet together. She had her right leg crossed behind the other. I could see no way to move without knocking her to the floor. We were all tangled up with no way out.

We stood there for a silly second. Sweat started to form on the back of my neck.

"Can I recommend something?"

Her breath was hot.

I sighed. "I think we're stuck."

"Yes," she said calmly. "But, with the tango, there's always a way out. You can dance your way out of any problem."

"I think you're accustomed to better dancers," I replied with a nervous laugh.

"No, no, no," she insisted, very serious. "This is easy. Just relax."

"Okay. What do I do?"

"All you have to do is shift your balance." She leaned in closer to me, her chest sinking further into mine, balancing herself on one foot while the other remained suspended in midair. "Just pass your weight to your left foot, and then you'll be able to lead me forward."

I played this out in my head. Could it really be that easy? Unlikely. But I had no other viable plan. Without changing my stance, I transferred my weight to my left foot. The shift was imperceptible; no one watching us could have noticed. Then, I rotated the axis of my shoulders clockwise and eased my right foot out of the way. She was now able to step forward, and voila, the day was saved. A miracle. My heart was pounding.

"You know, a lot of dancers do that shift on purpose," she whispered as we resumed our loop around the dance floor. "It's a very nice move. Personally, I adore it. A little thing, perhaps. But sometimes greatness is just the sum of many little things."

I smiled. "Should we try it again?"

"I think that's your decision."

Again: God bless the tango.

A few more steps, and I succeeded in getting us hopelessly stuck for round two. This time, I fanned out my right hand, like I had seen El Tigre do a million times, pulled her lower back closer to my torso, and shifted my weight. Again, she was able to walk right out of the trap.

"*Ay*," she sighed. "*Me parte la cabeza cuando hacen eso.*"

It blows my mind when they do that, she said. I tried to peek at her face out of the corner of my eye, but I could only see her bare back, and the tattoo. From up close, to my surprise, the scorpion appeared faded, sloppily rendered, the edges bleeding out a bit.

Just then, with a crash from the piano, the song ended. We lingered in the embrace for a long moment; I sure as hell wasn't going to end it. Finally, slowly, she pulled away.

"That was very nice," she said. A tiny smile was frozen on her face. "You dance very well."

"You're too kind," I said with a laugh, staring now at the floor, simultaneously embarrassed and pleased. "Really, I just started to learn tango recently."

"Are you taking classes?"

"Yes. At La Estrella."

"Ah. That's a nice place to learn. *Buena gente.* Good people."

"Yes."

"But if you ever decide you want private classes, I can give you my card."

"*You* give private tango classes?"

"Yes. I have a studio in San Telmo."

Rather coolly, I thought, I pretended to think about her offer for a moment. "That could be good," I mused out loud, as if I needed convincing. "Well, maybe I can call you."

"Please."

With the grace of a pickpocket, she removed a business card from somewhere, God knows where, inside her strapless dress.

"I'm Mariela. Call me."

And then, with a curtsy and a kiss on the cheek, she retreated to the bar.

An hour later, I found myself seated at a table toward the back of the dance hall by myself, despondently nursing a whisky. I had tried to follow up my tango with Mariela, eager to build on my unexpected success. But each of the other five or so women I'd danced with had proven a terrible disappointment. They were clumsy, they were overweight, they didn't smell as good, they didn't do what I told them to, and so on. These women were Yugos. Meanwhile, my Mercedes-Benz was still at the bar, laughing and drinking, and I stared without shame as man after man caught her eye and invited her to dance. She would smile, give the same curtsy, and then float around the dance floor with these other strangers, looking utterly poised and happy.

I ordered another whisky and stared at the floor, feeling completely lost and alone. I'll call her, I decided. Until then, I'd just have to spend the rest of the night drinking away that sudden strange, hollow feeling in my stomach, wherever the hell *that* had come from.

THE FOLLOWING FRIDAY NIGHT AT LA ESTRELLA, THE CROWD was unusually sparse. A special breed of unemployed protesters—*piqueteros*, they're called—had cut off roads all over the industrial ring of the city, setting up rows of burning tires and camping out right there on the concrete. They set up tents and soundstages and *ollas populares*, pots of stew from which everybody slowly ate during the day, building up enough endurance to stay on the highway for days, even weeks at a time. In most cases, they had only one demand: jobs. There were none to be had, of course; companies were firing people, and the Argentine government, for the first time in history, was unable to pick up the slack by padding its rolls with thousands upon thousands of *ñoquis*. Such was life in a country where unemployment was now at 25 percent. There hadn't yet been any *piquetero* roadblocks in *capi-*

tal federal—the federal district that was the central core of Buenos Aires—but everyone seemed to meekly agree it was just a matter of time before they went there, too.

I was still somewhat disconsolate from the experience with Mariela. I had tried dancing with a few other women but had found the experience completely unsatisfying. I was stuck at the table now with only El Gil and Juan El Negro, who was staring into his empty glass and idly pushing around peanuts on the table. I was completely shocked to realize that I had never actually seen the man dance.

"I once went fifty-seven years without dancing," he told me. "That was the length of time I was married to my wife. I had danced as an adolescent, but I married very young. We stayed at home, we raised our kids—there was no need for tango. And then, two years ago, you know, she passed. I was trapped at home. My nostalgia was killing me. I couldn't be in my house, yet I didn't want to leave. Then El Nene Patterson came over . . . you know El Nene?" I nodded. "El Nene made me come back to the milonga, and he made me dance." He sighed and rubbed his eyes. "At first, I didn't want to. I thought I was betraying my wife by dancing with other people. But El Nene and my other friends insisted I needed to get out, to see people. The doctor said the same. So I went first to the Confiteria Ideal, then to Salon Canning, then I started coming here to La Viruta. I danced with one, then another, and before long, I found that I couldn't stop."

"That's marvelous," I said.

But the story didn't end there, and Juan El Negro's winning smile quickly faded. "They've introduced me to a few women," he said softly. "But I didn't want to redo my life. It would be bad for everyone. Because I'm dead in here," he said, pointing to his chest. "If I got a girlfriend, I'd kill her—not literally, of course, but . . . you know what I mean to say. Sometimes I start crying, and *me agarra un ataque de mi mujer*—I get an attack of my wife—and I can't function. I met a girl; we went out for a little bit. But my nostalgia for my wife was destroying her, and we had to break up. Now, she comes twice a week," he said, nodding to an attractive middle-aged woman in a black dress, sitting a few tables over. "She looks at me. I look at her. I think she wants to give it another try. But I can't take her out anymore. I just can't.

"There's no point," he reasoned. "With my wife, we met at a stop for the trolley. Six months later, we got engaged and married. We spent fifty-seven years completely *enamorados*. So let's say I meet somebody new now. Do I stop loving my wife? Do I destroy the new one? Am I that big of a coward?

"El Nene tells me, 'You're still young.' I can't think that way. I have a friend, a colonel, who told me the same thing. Then, he lost his wife. Now he understands, he tells me I'm right. You move on, but you never forget."

The crowd seemed to have thinned even further, even though it was only 2 A.M.

"Anyway," he added, almost as an afterthought, "the milonga is not nearly as glorious as it used to be."

I took the bait. "How so?"

"It's all so automated now," he said. "Back when I was learning—this was 1946 and 1947—all the *muchachos* from the neighborhood would come over to our house, which had a patio. My old lady would let them in, and we would dance. If there was a woman, fine, but if not we would dance among ourselves. If a guy had a new step, he would teach. The other would be the woman.

"When Perón took charge, the young people started going out. Everything changed. Before that, we had to do everything in the shadows. I'm not a politician, or in a union or anything. But when Perón took charge, things changed, the country changed."

El Gil piped up: "Whoever denies that is an idiot. Perón gave us everything."

"The government gave out shoes," Juan added. "They were ugly, but they worked. People who were not part of society suddenly were. Movies, for example. Before Perón, you had to have a suit jacket, a *saco*, to enter theaters. That was the law. After Perón, no, you could go with normal dress. That sounds trivial today. Now, in Argentina, the fourteen-year-old is sitting at a bar drinking whiskey with his parents. But these things, they were important six decades ago."

Something—Perón, the memory of the theaters, the mere thought of 1946—had now thawed Juan El Negro's melancholy, and his voice had become stronger, younger. "Before I met my wife, I took a woman out once to dance the tango," he said. "She was beautiful, an ample chest. You understand? All my friends desired her. A friend of mine walked over to us and ordered us to stop dancing. He told the girl to come talk with him. I said, 'No, she has to come with me.' All of a sudden, the son of a bitch kicked me in the knee. It was a dirty blow. So he won the first round.

"For the second round, we went downstairs. There, I kicked his ass. Then I took my girl to a restaurant and I had a giant *milanesa* steak." He turned to El Gil. "Do you remember how big the *milanesas* were back then?"

"Ah yes," El Gil said, "*las milanesas en ese entonces eran muy grandes.*"

"So, I get up to go to the bathroom again, and there he is. I said, 'Do you want to finish this, motherfucker?' He said yes, and we went over to the obelisk. . . . "

"The obelisk?" I exclaimed, surprised. He was referring to the phallus reminiscent of the Washington Monument in the middle of downtown Buenos Aires.

"Yes."

"Why the obelisk?"

"We were looking for someplace symbolic." He laughed. "I don't know. Anyhow, we went to the obelisk and he spit on the ground and I spit on him and then we beat the shit out of each other. It was difficult to beat me back then. *Yo era boxeador como la gran puta.* I used to box like a motherfucker. And, I tell you, I kicked his ass!"

Juan sat there in silence for a moment, hyperventilating with nostalgia. "Things never came of any consequence during those times, though. A few days passed, and we were friends again. It wasn't like today. Today, with all these *negros* out there on the road, blocking traffic and *haciendo mierda*," he seethed, "there's no way for an honest man to live. These savages, the politicians rent them to do their bidding, they make them beg for money. It's like 'Cambalache' says: 'he who doesn't cry, doesn't nurse.' The uncivilized animals are eating this country apart. Soon there will be no Argentina at all."

I sat there, stunned. It was the most astonishing tour de force of pessimism I had ever heard in my life. And it wasn't quite over:

"What does it matter," he snorted, getting up to leave. "I'll die soon anyway."

WHEN HE WASN'T BUSY GALLOPING ABOUT THE PAMPA WITH the gauchos, G. Whitfield Ray had the not-so-unusual privilege of witnessing an armed revolt against an Argentine president. On July 26, 1890, thousands of men swarmed the streets of Buenos Aires chanting "*Sangre! Sangre!* Blood! Blood!" as they demanded the resignation of the punching-bag of the hour, one Don Juarez Celman. Trenches were dug in the streets, ragtag bands performed martial music (if they played "Stars and Stripes Forever," Ray did not say), and the low, flat rooftops were quickly filled with snipers. "Men mounted their steeds with a careless laugh," Ray wrote, "while the rising sun shone on their burnished arms, so soon to be stained with blood."

In the inevitable battle, over a thousand people lost their lives. As soon as the shooting stopped, Ray went for a long walk and saw wounded soldiers still in the field, "ravenously eating the dead horses which strewed the streets. Some were lying down to drink the water flowing in the gutters, which was often tinged with human blood. . . . There were men to all appearances fast asleep, standing with their arms in the reins of the horses which had borne them safely through the leaden hail of that day of terror."

History has since forgotten Celman—he is one of the only Argentine presidents for whom I don't recall ever seeing a statue or even a bust—and the Revolution of 1890 would soon be dwarfed by the far more dramatic revolutions of the century to come. Years later, though, Ray still seemed bewildered by the peculiar nature of revolution in Argentina.

"Men looted the stores and feasted," he wrote. "Lawless hordes visited the police offices, threw their furniture into the streets, tore to shreds all the books, papers, and records found, and created general havoc."

During that same era, an Englishman named A. Stuart Pennington, who had spent two decades living in Argentina (thus becoming one of the first real *anglo-argentinos*), wrote with marked nostalgia: "The Gaucho race is slowly dying out. The wild horse still roams the plains and the lasso is still used to throw the animal . . . but the times have changed and the race is changing with them, and the Gaucho will ere-long be only a legend in the heroic history of the country."

By the turn of the century, Pennington's prophecy had largely come true. The reasons for the gaucho's demise are no mystery—much as happened to the cowboy; his good life of limitless meat and wide-open spaces was inevitably crushed by what some people deemed progress. Huge tracts of prime real estate on the Pampa were given as spoils of war to the same Argentine generals who had once employed gauchos as soldiers. Gratitude had its limits, though; these generals would become Argentina's new elite, and they were the most zealous in closing off their properties to the free-roaming gauchos. The ideas of Spanish feudalism still lived among the Argentine colonists of a century before. Barbed wire was rolled out, the range was fenced in, and one by one, cattle pastures across Argentina became rolling fields of wheat.

G. Whitfield Ray had commented that the gauchos were thoroughly worthless at commercial agriculture. Maybe they were merely disinterested; the farming lifestyle was too sedentary, the labor was too backbreaking, and also it was too easy for the women to keep tabs on them. With no other viable options, and with their meat supplies suddenly running low, the resigned gauchos streamed unhappily into the outskirts of Buenos Aires, the *arrabales*. Here, their lifestyles would become more urban, their knives would become (slightly) shorter in length, and they and their offspring would soon be known not as gauchos but as *compadritos*, men from the Pampa who had little skill as workers but who proved tremendously useful as petty criminals and as armies of thugs for political bosses.

In those days, the line between Buenos Aires and the Pampa was still very blurred. One visitor described the city as a "repulsive barnyard"; the naturalist W. H. Hudson deemed it "a city of evil smells." For three centuries the city had subsisted almost entirely as an illegal smuggling haven, trading in salted meat and cowhide, and some silver every now and then; it was a forgotten corner of the Spanish Empire that had gained its independence, almost reluctantly, in 1810. When the gauchos trudged in, Buenos Aires was still part pirate port, part stockyard, part fortress against the Indians. It was one of the only cities in the world where beggars charged about on horseback, extending their tin collection cup with one hand, and pulling in the horse's reins with the other. Fish vendors walked through the streets, their catch suspended from thick bamboo sticks they carried across their shoulders. Armadillo was also a favorite dish, tasty although "not very prepossessing in appearance at the table," a British visitor noted. Chickens were raised on the roofs of buildings, which were uniformly pink or green and squattish and thoroughly undesirable. Property was worth next to nothing; it was said that a huge chunk of central Buenos Aires had been sold for nothing more than a white horse and a guitar.

At each extreme of the city there was a *matadero*, a slaughterhouse, where a few compadritos and gauchos could sometimes find nominally reputable work. It was the age before industrial slaughter: Cattle were released one by one from a *corralito*, and then it was up to the workers to lasso them, throw them on the ground, and slash their throats with a knife. In this manner, the entire herd was slaughtered, their carcasses left on the dusty ground until all were dead. Then, the workers swapped their knives for axes and set about hacking the beef into manageable pieces. This may have provoked sheer nostalgia among the gauchos and their kin, but "to a foreigner," wrote one visitor, "nothing can be more disgusting than the mode of supplying this place with beef." The wind whipped the leftovers all through the city, and buildings everywhere were covered with a fine silt of Pampa mud and cattle guts. It is thus understandable that the city provoked a disgust among visitors that was almost comic in its intensity. Lucio Mansilla, an Argentine diplomat and writer who had been educated in the somewhat less dusty universities of Europe, described his hometown as nothing more than a "vertiginous agitation, in the middle of narrow, muddy, dirty, fetid streets that block out the horizon and the clean, pure sky . . . all crowded together by egoism, like a bunch of disgusting shell fish." And he was being kind.

It wasn't the Paris of South America, no, not quite yet—the frontier town was popularly known instead as *la gran aldea*, "the great village." What wealth did exist was precarious at best. There *was* an opera house, but before setting out for a performance on a rainy night, wealthy porteños first had to check the sky to see if a flag was flying from a building downtown. If the flag was up, then the streets of the city were washed out and impassable, and thus the opera was canceled. This happened often in a city that received substantially more precipitation per year (39 inches) than rainy old London (30 inches). And mud was merely a minor challenge to a civilized night out; there were also pickpockets, drunks, and the odd leering gaucho. It must have been a tremendously lonely life; here people were, in an outpost on the edge of the wild Pampa, thousands of miles away from Europe, often unable to do so much as take a dignified stroll down the street. The sidewalks were little more than wooden slats, and crossing the street sometimes meant stepping over the decomposing remains of dead horses that had been pushed over to the side of the road. Ray wrote: "I have seen delicate ladies, attired in Parisian furbelows, lift their dainty skirts, attempt the crossing—and sink in a mass of corruption, full of maggots."

No wonder, then, that the emerging elite in Buenos Aires were so eager to cut any ties with the past. The Argentine intellectuals of the era saw their country as a struggle between *civilizacion* and *barbarie*—and victory had to be won at any cost. Domingo F. Sarmiento, a president during the 1880s who had traveled widely in the United States (and is maybe the only leader in the country's history whom modern-day Argentines can all agree did an acceptable job), implemented mandatory and free education. Sarmiento also decided that the path to civilization was in bringing immigrants from Europe, preferably from northern regions like England or Scandinavia, so that they could teach the sons of gauchos their "civilized" ways. The new Argentina would be urban, cultured, and white—and everybody else would be domesticated, like it or not. "The gauchos simply did not figure in the liberal dream of Europeanization and progress," wrote the historian Nicolas Shumway in his book *The Invention of Argentina*. "They were ignored, outcast, and marginal; necessary only for rigging and elections and fighting wars."

Just as the last gauchos were trudging into the cities, the literary poem *Martin Fierro* was published—an event as important to Argentine culture as the release of *Don Quixote* is to Spain's. The book's publication received scant notice in Buenos Aires, but its first printing sold out within two months in the Pampa. *Martin Fierro*, about a gaucho by the same name, was essentially a heartbreaking tale of closing fences. Many gauchos—unable to read, of course—committed the poem to memory. It was their *Iliad*. In the book, Fierro rebels against the evil central government in Buenos Aires, which dared to curtail the gauchos' freedom by tricking them into military service.

> *A gaucho'd live in his home country*
> *As safe as anything.*
> *But now—it's a crime!*
> *Things have got to be so twisted*
> *That a poor man wears out his life*
> *Running from the authorities.*

Fierro went during his travels "to see the milonga," but in the end, his was not a happy journey. At the conclusion of *Martin Fierro*, the two main characters—both gauchos—give up and decide to leave Argentina forever and live among the Indians where "the powers of government don't reach." In one last outburst, Fierro smashes his guitar into a thousand pieces, and then, in the poem's final stanza, the

two gauchos cross the border and look back on the last
Argentine village while:

> *Two big tears went rolling*
> *Down Martin Fierro's face.*

And if that doesn't sound like a tango, what does?

I HAD SPENT COUNTLESS HOURS AS A TEENAGER LISTENING
to George Strait and Willie Nelson (yes, I also drove a red
pickup truck), so, given that I had come to Argentina in part
to get as far away from Texas as possible, it was a bit discon-
certing to realize that El Dandy was right: there were clear
parallels between the tango and the country music. The gaucho and the cowboy had many of the same matters on their
minds. In his classic 1975 country music hit "You Never
Even Called Me by My Name," David Allan Coe made a list
of the topics that would be touched on by the perfect country music song: mama, trucks, prison, trains, and "gettin'
drunk." Just about every tango meets at least one of those
criteria, including at least fourteen songs with the word
"mama" in the title. And while it's hard to imagine Garth
Brooks performing a song quite as nakedly hyperbolic as
"*Madre*," a tango first performed in 1922 . . . :

> *Mother,*
> *The sadness sunk me,*
> *And I cried without your love.*

When the night flooded me
With my profound pain.
Mother,
There is no more sublime love
Nor a greater saint for me.

. . . many of the tangos about booze and cheating do have a distinctly familiar ring:

Crazy illusions
Vain illusions
Dragged me around blindly
In my youth.
In gambling houses, milongas
And distant good times
Where I left
My good health.

It is not hard to imagine Johnny Cash crooning these lyrics. The tango might not possess quite as strong a Wild West, frontier flavor as that heard (and seen) in country music, but it is still unmistakably present. Replace the Colt .45 with a dagger, the cowboy hat with a slightly cocked derby, and the transformation from Hank Williams to Carlos Gardel was nearly complete. In fact, I might have accepted El Dandy's claim that the gauchos were solely responsible for inventing the tango—were it not for one fundamental, hugely important fact that I remembered from my pickup-truck days.

When I was growing up, my dad lived about thirty-five miles north of Dallas in a small Texas town called Celina. I visited on weekends. The town had seventeen hundred people, a championship football team (the Bobcats), a gas station (the Bobkat Kuntry), and a small greasy-spoon restaurant (the Bobcat Café) that was run by friends of ours. Above all, I remember two things about the Bobcat Café: (1) Friday was steak night, featuring a T-bone, a side, and dessert for $9.99; and (2) country music was summarily *banned* from the boom-box radio in the kitchen. Why? Because the owner thought the music was too sad. Hours and hours of steel guitars and fiddles were enough to drive the cooks and waitresses to the brink of insanity; there had been several cases of people breaking down in tears. For the sake of a healthy workplace, there could be no Reba McEntire.

This is where the genres diverge: Tango lyrics are sad. Tango *music* is not. In fact, a person who does not understand Spanish might listen to a few songs and conclude that the tango is meant to be happy. The interplay of the piano, strings, and *bandoneon* is often lively, even jovial. The gaucho, even if his happy-go-lucky side is accounted for, could not have produced such music by himself. All signs point to a missing influence, something present during the early days before lyrics were introduced, that gave tango a more playful and optimistic spirit.

The answer would shock most Argentines. The clues lie in the multiple theories as to the origin of the word "tango." Perhaps more than any other single group, people of African descent had an enormous impact on tango music and the dance. This is jarring, because as anyone who has ever visited Argentina knows, there is almost no visible African presence on the streets. One can spend months in Buenos Aires and never see a single person who would traditionally be described as black.

In fact, the sight is so rare that porteños will often point and stare when a black tourist walks by. In closer quarters, black foreigners are normally treated, though politely, as an exotic phenomenon. As night fell at a rooftop party one evening, an African American woman who is a friend of mine was told by a grinning Argentine man: "*Está tan oscuro que casi no te veo—* It's so dark out here I can barely see you." ("I think he meant it as a pick-up line!" she recalled, bewildered.) Walk through the Museo Nacional de Bellas Artes, the closest thing Argentina has to a flagship museum, and you see portraits of upper-class families and picturesque country scenes of sturdy gauchos; their complexions range from porcelain white to little darker than a rugged tan, but—to the shock of no one—there are no blacks depicted.

So, consider this: as recently as the 1840s, *one third* of Buenos Aires' population was of African descent. How they almost completely disappeared in the years thereafter is one of the great historical mysteries in a country chock full of mysteries. Today, only a vague memory of their existence lingers, manifesting itself in jokes, paranoid rumors, and innuendo. An elderly Argentine comedian, Tato Bores, began his TV show by asking, "Where did all the *negros* go?" Few other Argentines know to even ask the question.

While Argentina was never a major center of the slave trade like Brazil or the United States—there were no plantations, no cash crops like cotton to be cultivated on the as yet untapped Pampa—it did import several thousand African slaves during the early nineteenth century. They were mostly urban servants, maids and doormen, tailors and street-sweepers. Buenos Aires also had a relatively high population of free blacks; many of them lived in San Telmo, then known as *el barrio del tambor*, or the neighborhood of the drum. Today, it is the center of the porteño tango scene. The blacks had a vibrant community but one that was always somewhat under siege, and—like that of the gauchos—did not jibe with the Argentine elite's vision of forging a white, European country.

Dance was (and is) a hugely important part of African culture, and the blacks of Buenos Aires performed a ritual called *candombe* that anthropologists believe was a direct predecessor of the tango. By the mid-nineteenth century, the white elites had banned overtly African dances from the streets. Here again, we come back to a possible genesis of "tango"—in certain African tongues, the word means "closed place" or "reserved ground," which makes sense if the dance was driven underground. As blacks were freed, they needed to earn a living, and they fell back on the unique skills they had. Thus, by the 1850s, the first *academias de baile* began to appear.

The embryonic tango was nurtured in these so-called dance academies, where white Argentines could pay a small fee and drink the night away. It is thought that the earliest tangos were danced by *compadritos*, or latter-day, urbanized gauchos, who performed an imprecise imitation, or a mockery, of the African dance, or *candombe*, they saw. (Even then, Argentine creativity was centered in satire and cynicism. Nothing has changed.) The *academias* were also frequented by young men of the porteño elite who were on the prowl in lower-class neighborhoods (these days, this would be called slumming) and notorious for shattering streetlights, breaking windows, and destroying furniture after a night of dancing. Over time, they took tango back to their houses, dancing it with their friends in secret because their parents had strictly forbidden it. This type of spoiled, rich young man, instrumental in the spread of the tango's popularity, soon came to be known in porteño slang as a *niño bien*.

Historians do not know precisely what happened to the city's black community. There are several theories; each of them probably contains a kernel of truth, and none paint Argentine history in a particularly heartwarming light. The most common theory holds that most of the city's blacks were conscripted into the Argentine army and then put on the front lines in a war against Paraguay in the 1860s. There they perished in disproportionate numbers. The yellow fever epidemic that struck Buenos Aires in the 1860s had its deadliest effects in neighborhoods such as San Telmo where the proportion of ethnic African people was highest. Many blacks may have sensed they were no longer welcome and emigrated to places like Brazil and neighboring Uruguay. Those blacks that remained were overwhelmed by the wave of European immigration that began in the 1880s. By the mid-twentieth century there were only about two thousand Afro-Argentines left in Buenos Aires.

Still, their influence was enormous. At least thirty-five black musicians played tango in Buenos Aires from 1890 to 1930, according to the Yale art historian Robert F. Thompson, who wrote a magisterial book that fully chronicles the African influence on the tango. Celedonio Flores, considered by many to be the first great composer of tango lyrics, was of black origin. Thompson also draws a parallel between the trash-talking, chest-pounding, self-inflating lyrics of some tangos with the same tone in American hip-hop music. As late as the 1970s, there was still a place, called the Shimmy Club, where the black community gathered to dance and socialize.

Today, Argentines scoff at the notion that their country could have any African roots, but the evidence is present if one knows where to look. Thompson provides a long list of words unique to Argentine Spanish that he says come directly from Africa—among them is *mucama*, the term for "maid," which in the language of the Congo means "royal mistress of a house." (The rich old Argentine ladies bossing their maids around in Barrio Norte would surely have blanched with embarrassment if they had known what they were saying.) Even more prominent is the presence of African bloodlines, if barely, in many Argentines; it is entirely plausible, for example, that El Tigre had some black ancestors. I asked him about this once. His response: "Don't be a fool." He didn't speak to me for the rest of the night. In a country where anyone with a hint of skin pigmentation is called *un negro* and where whiter people tend to be richer people, it was hard to blame him for being paranoid. This is why debates over the past can become so vehement in Argentina, why men like El Dandy seem ready to fight to the death to defend their version of history. It is a country that has never been at ease with its true identity and where decades of decline mean that each Argentine has his or her own theory as to when and how things went wrong. After all, porteños today are dancing a black dance in a city that used to be full of black people—yet almost no one has any idea. That's Argentina for you.

part three

TWICE WITHOUT
PULLING OUT

THE DOOR WAS ANSWERED BY A GRIMACING GRANDMOTHER in a tattered red flannel nightgown. My poorly concealed look of dismay seemed to register with her, and she accepted it with a resigned smirk. Definitely not the first time she'd had to deal with men like me, it seemed. She rolled her eyes and motioned for me to come inside.

She showed me to a kitchen that was dark and smelled of burnt coffee grounds. Dozens of dirty dishes were scattered around the room. The old lady had a dishrag slung over her arm, as if promising she'd get around to washing them one of these years. A flickering TV on a cart played Bugs Bunny cartoons dubbed into Spanish. On the floor, a teenage boy was stretched out in a sleeping bag, facing away from me.

"*Hola,*" I ventured.

He waved his hand around in the air, not bothering to look back.

The old lady gestured for me to sit down. Not a word from her yet. Apparently they were accustomed to mute foreigners around here.

I waited.

"¡*Qué pato más tonto!*" Bugs Bunny said.

Finally, the door into the adjacent room swung open.

"You can come in, Bruno."

Mariela stood there waiting, alone. She looked absolutely nothing like the woman I remembered from a few nights before. Now, in the light of morning, she was wearing torn blue jeans, ballet slippers, and a low-cut soft-pink blouse. The scorpion was artfully concealed. She had applied no lipstick and light black circles were just perceptible under her eyes. She was still very pretty, of course, but all the polish, all the meticulous gloss from the other night—it was gone, vanished, replaced by something much more uncertain. She recognized me and smiled, sincerely but without enthusiasm, as if not entirely convinced she wanted to be there. As we stood and stared at each other, she lightly traced a figurine on the floor with her ballet slipper, looking suddenly very fragile, waiting for me to say the first word.

I felt a sudden impulse to run. But I resisted, determined to re-create *that* feeling—whatever the hell it was—that I had experienced the other night, long after midnight at the Niño Bien.

First, though, there was the little matter of my name.

"It's Brian," I said, trying to be as nonchalant as possible. "Not Bruno."

"Oh," she replied nervously. "I'm sorry. We were out dancing until dawn."

For some reason, this made me feel better.

Mariela had set up her dance studio on the ground floor of her house, in a brick-walled room with three finely finished French windows that grandly opened out to the street. The studio was modestly decorated, bereft of the film noir posters of dancing couples that some milongas depended on to manufacture a sense of mystery and melodrama. An antique lamp shone a muted, golden light from above, and a sturdy ceiling fan whipped through the thick air. A few telltale signs suggested that this was a successful endeavor: There was a video camera mounted on a tripod over in the corner, and even a DVD player—the first one I'd seen in Argentina—hooked up to an incongruously ancient Noblex television, a relic from the old days when Argentina still made its own TVs. On the other side of the room was a clothes rack with an array of sequined leotards and dark blazers (perfect for a Broadway show but thoroughly ridiculous for Buenos Aires) with a sign in English only that read: FOR SALE.

She walked over to a little CD jukebox in the corner and pressed Play. A soft, scratchy recording of a slow tango came on. Then she sauntered over to me and smiled—a real one, this time—and, without saying a word, she held up her arms, inviting me to dance.

I stepped into the embrace and swallowed uneasily. This had felt more natural the other night, when we were surrounded by a mix of music and booze and sex; now I felt like I was in a laboratory, being examined. By the fourth step, I had completely forgotten everything I had learned. My head felt like it was sinking; my arms felt like they weighed two tons each. I ended up performing the same *paso básico*, the same seven-step sequence I had learned that night at La Estrella, the curse of my existence, over and over until the song came to a merciful end.

"Very good!" she exclaimed. "Why are you even here?"

"Excuse me?"

"You don't need any classes. You dance very well!"

I felt certain she was patronizing me, but I didn't know what to say.

"So why are you here? What is your problem?"

"Well," I said, slowly, "I don't really *feel* the tango."

A bewildered pause.

"Excuse me?" she said.

"I feel like I dance too mechanically," I continued. "It's like I'm not really feeling whatever the tango is all about."

"Very interesting," she mused. She looked at me differently now, as if I represented a problem she hadn't seen before, like a doctor faced with an entirely new and exotic ailment from the Amazon. "That *is* complicated."

"So what do we do?" I asked.

"The tango is passion. It's transmitted from one person to another, but it's also a passion for the dance. Are you a passionate person?"

The question seemed important, but I had no idea how to answer it. "I think so."

Mariela chewed on her fingernails for a moment, possessed by a new nervous energy. Whatever else, I had shaken her from her apparent boredom. "What *exactly* do you think about when you tango?"

"I feel like tango is just a sequence of numbers, and that I'm constantly repeating variations of them instead of actually enjoying myself and, you know, dancing."

"Hmm. That's very perceptive, actually." She briskly walked over to a dry erase board hanging from the wall, picked up a marker, and wrote:

1-3
5-2
6-3
7-2
7-3

"Do you recognize this?" she asked, pointing.

The numbers were in chicken-scratch handwriting, like the scientific equations of a mad professor. I wondered: is this a dance or is it nuclear physics?

"It seems familiar," I said, "in a terrible sort of way."

She smiled with something resembling sympathy. "The *paso basico* is really seven steps, and you can do variations. You don't have to do them all in order, though, one through seven. You can mix them up—like I've written here—and they'll seem like completely different steps. . . . "

At that moment, through the window in the door, I spotted someone else in the kitchen. The glass was partially obscured by a white lace doily, but I could definitely make out someone—probably male, older, and somewhat short, it appeared—sitting there eating, what, a bowl of cereal? Who was this guy, the next student? Was my class already over? We had begun a half-hour late. Overcome by panic, I started brainstorming. How could I squeeze at least an extra fifteen minutes out of the class?

And then, it suddenly dawned on me what she had said about the night before.

"*We?*"

Unaware that she had completely lost my attention, Mariela was methodically wrapping up her standard lecture on the finer points of the *paso básico*. "My point is that you shouldn't feel imprisoned," she said with a wry smile. "Tango was originally invented as an expression of liberty, you know."

I laughed.

"It's simple. You can do them in any order. Steps 1 through 4 are the *caminata*, and 6 through 8 are the *resolución*. Number 5 is the *stop*." She paused and smiled. "And that's the only English you'll ever hear out of me. So why don't we stop talking and try a few of these variations? We can try the 7 to 3, first."

This actually made some sense. We waited for a new song to start, I pulled her in, and we gave it our best go. Skipping from 7 to 3 was really nothing more complex than skipping the last step of the normal cycle, and moving forward instead of moving sideways. This sounds laughably basic. But given that I only had a repertoire of two moves at the time, adding a third seemed like a divine revelation.

The moment the song ended, the door swung open. It was the old lady, who had changed into an oddly exuberant flower-print dress and was now staring intently, perhaps protectively, at Mariela.

"I'm going out for milk," she said, "and my feet hurt."

"Okay. Thanks, Grandma," Mariela chirped. She considered this for a moment, like something hadn't quite been right, and then her attention shifted back to me. No music was playing now, but we were still embraced in midstep. I imagined that we looked like two teenagers making out on a dark street. She smiled at me warmly, genuinely and rubbed her hand on my back, massaging me a bit. Her eyes were sharp, her gaze attentive; like she was awaiting some kind of order. "So how are you feeling now, Brian?"

"Fine. Better."

She lightly squeezed my left shoulder. "Does this hurt?"

To my surprise, it did.

"I thought so," she beamed, pleased with her diagnostic ability. The doctor at work. "You poor thing. Your body shouldn't hurt. All the movement in the tango should be completely natural, as easy as walking. If your legs hurt, if your shoulder hurts, then you're doing something wrong. You need to relax. Don't let all that tension build in your upper body." She winked, then added with a teasing, sly grin: "I know you're strong. You don't have to prove it to me, you know."

The door opened again. This time, in walked a man who appeared to be in his midthirties. His was clearly the silhouette from the breakfast table. He wore shorts and flip-flops, was unshaven, and looked like he had just rolled out of bed—even though it was already 2 P.M. He strolled confidently over to us, nodded perfunctorily at me, lightly pulled Mariela out of our embrace, and gave her a big, wet, authoritative kiss on the lips.

"*Buen día, querida,*" he murmured.

"*Buen día. Daniel, te presento a Brian.*"

"*Mucho gusto,*" I said, shaking his hand, struggling to keep my eyes from bursting out of my head. "*¿Cómo le va?*"

Daniel was three inches shorter than Mariela, maybe ten years her senior, and weighed no more than 150 pounds when wet. He had a compact, professional dancer's body with a puffed-out chest and a perfect stride, exerting flawless control over each and every movement he made. With a subtle flicker of his gaze, he looked me up and down—and, based on that one expert evaluation, it seemed he could have recited my weight, body-fat percentage, and age with the accuracy of a carnival barker. He had a kind smile, bright eyes; he was handsome, poised, and good-natured. I hated him the instant I saw him.

"*Un placer,*" he said, bowing courteously.

"We've been working on the seven steps," Mariela reported. "7 to 3."

Daniel turned to her and cocked his head, as if surprised. "So soon? Does he dance well?"

"Yes. He needs some work, but he seems to move well enough. He has bad posture that needs improvement, but that should happen if he dances enough. His embrace has a certain hunchbacked quality. . . . "

They were talking about me as if I wasn't there—in quiet tones, but making no effort not to be heard. I was too bewildered to be offended.

". . . though some basic exercises should address that as well. The biggest hurdle will be psychological. He seems to know music. In sum, I think there is potential."

"*Muy bien, adelante,*" Daniel concluded. The bastard winked at me. "Good luck! See you next week!"

After that, we wordlessly danced a few more tangos, trying the blessed 7–3 step a few dozen more times. Puddles of sweat appeared under her arms.

Then, abruptly, she pulled away, shrugged, and stared expectantly at me.

"What?" I asked.

"The class is over."

"Oh."

She was still staring. My eyes drifted over to the window.

"So. . . ."

"The money?" she asked, with barely a whisper.

"Ah, of course," I blurted, embarrassed. I reached into my pocket and pulled out a soggy twenty-peso bill.

Mariela smiled with relief, thrust the money into her front pocket, and happily escorted me out to the street.

"Remember what I said about passion," she chirped, swinging open the door. "That seems to be what brings people to the tango. Yes, that seems to be what happens. There was an Italian here for two months," she said wistfully. "When it was all over, I asked him, 'What did you see of Buenos Aires?' And he said, only this street. Because he stayed at a hostel ten houses down," she smiled, "and the poor little guy was so *impassioned* that he spent his entire vacation just going back and forth between the hostel and the studio. It was all he wanted to do. Isn't that funny?"

Poor guy, I thought, as I turned away to walk down the street. He never stood a chance.

ON THOSE RARE NIGHTS WHEN I DIDN'T GO TO THE MI-longa, I would come home from the office and pan-fry a steak (yes, this was sacrilege) while listening to the radio. I was almost always eager to get a break from the melancholy of Gardel and Trolio, so I would listen to something else— usually melancholy American pop music from the 1980s. There were in fact four all-'80s FM radio stations in Buenos

Aires that played a steady diet of Lionel Ritchie, Madonna (just the really old stuff: "Like a Virgin" as opposed to "Like a Prayer"), The Cars, and every other overwrought artist or group that I had grown up listening to in my mom's minivan. Something about '80s music appealed to the porteño soul in the same way tango did. The venerable 94.7 Horizonte was the most reliably sappy station, having a special zeal for Neal Diamond and A-ha; sadly (but perhaps for the good of mankind), the station did not survive the crisis. To this day, the song that reminds me the most of Buenos Aires is not a tango but "Broken Wings" by Mr. Mister.

One frigid evening at home, I was in the mood for tango. It had been a particularly trying day at work—there had been yet another sell-off on the stock exchange, and President De la Rúa had announced more cuts in pension plans—so I suppose I was in the mood to wallow a bit. This was an entirely new state of mind for me; I had never really experienced the urge to wallow before moving to Argentina, but I suppose this was about the time when I was starting to really go native. All the good tango stations were on the AM frequency, which involved hunting around with the dial on the old analog radio that was in the kitchen. I finally honed in on a good station, and the lyrics came in bitter and clear:

> I gave you a home.
> I was always poor, but I gave you a home.
> My combative smiles were spent
> Fighting for you,
> Bleeding for you.
> Truly, it's like scraping my palate with sand
> And choking without being able to scream.

I gave you a home. . . . It was love's fault!
It makes me want to shoot myself in a corner!

The next song was even more pronounced in its bile:

The future. . . . Why should I care about the future?
My whole life is yesterday.

At that point, I decided I'd had my fix. Enough self-pity. I played with the dial for a moment and ended up moving down a few notches to Radio 10, the popular talk radio station that taxi drivers listened to all day.

"*I can't stand the misery anymore,*" one of the callers was saying. "*Our children have grown up but have never known joy. Our country is worse than ever but there is nothing we can do to fix it.*"

This was too much. I flipped back to the tango station.

My Buenos Aires, dear land where my life will end.
Under your protection, there are no disappointments.
The years fly by, and pain is forgotten.
The memories pass like a caravan down a trail of sweet emotion.
I want to you to know that, upon invoking you,
The pain in my heart disappears. . . .
My dear Buenos Aires,
When I see you again, there will be no more pain or obscurity.

By now, I was laughing out loud. Back to Radio 10.

"*There is nothing good about Argentina today. Fifty years ago, we lived with dignity. Now there are only thieves and the honest people earn nothing. . . .*"

Argentines spoke in tango lyrics. I had come to this conclusion some time before. But what was incredible to me
now was how, with each passing day, life in Argentina was
becoming more and more like "Cambalache." The same bitter hopelessness, the same unshakeable melancholy, was
spreading throughout the country like a cancer. In fact, it was
often tempting to blame all the country's problems on some
kind of collective psychosis, as if Argentina had fallen under
some kind of spell. The new economy minister—the third
man to hold the job in just three weeks—had done precisely
that; at a press conference upon taking office, Domingo
Cavallo dismissively described the crisis as nothing more
than "a depression of the state of mind." Cavallo believed
that a shot of general optimism would be enough to reverse
the country's fortunes, and some scientific studies seemed to
suggest he might be on to something. Suicide rates were up;
so was impotence; so were domestic abuse and divorce.
People were sleeping less. Had everybody just gone crazy?
Even in the good—okay, the less bad—times, Buenos Aires
had been home to one of the world's highest concentrations
of psychoanalysts (the shrinks were doing fabulous business
because of the crisis). Maybe the tango had somehow con-
tributed to this disease by making self-pity glamorous and
mainstream—some Americans blamed gangsta rap for glori-
fying and thus perpetuating street violence, didn't they?
Wasn't music capable of not only reflecting but also changing popular culture? After all, Radio Horizonte was going
bankrupt, so it wasn't Rick Astley or the Human League
who were making Argentina's economy contract 3 percent a
year; to quote Luis, the owner of the Niño Bien, the milongas
were the only growth industry in Argentina.

In some aspects, this made sense—tango was the national music. It was logical for the country to turn to its roots at a time of crisis. But there was one thing that completely baffled me: with very few exceptions, no new tangos had been written for half a century. The tango's golden age had taken place between 1910 and 1950—the peak of Argentina's prosperity. Why had such astonishingly sad songs been written during a period of such unparalleled euphoria? And why had Argentina spent the next half-century basically living up to the lyrics?

None of it made sense. I flipped off the radio, plopped down on the sofa, and watched Crónica until 1 A.M. A protest was taking place outside the Ministry of Social Development. Some of the demonstrators were sobbing. Others jumped up and down like hooligans at a soccer match.

Around that same time, I realized my hair was falling out.

HIGH LIFE IN BUENOS AIRES! HIGH LIFE IN THE PARIS OF South America, where millionaires are thicker than blackberries in August and honey-lipped heiresses swarm like bees in midsummer!" enthused Frank G. Carpenter, an American journalist who visited Argentina just as the twentieth century, that most wicked cambalache of centuries, was about to begin. "We may see the high life out driving in the park of Palermo, or meet it every afternoon on the Calle Florida. We may take chances with it every Sunday at the races, or we may stare at its diamonds every night during the opera season. If we have good introductions we may go inside its mansions and attend its fine dinners, or perhaps take part in a game at the Jockey Club, where fortunes often change hands in a night."

Yes, this was Argentina just as the tango was on the verge of entering its golden era. Carpenter was not the type to be easily impressed; he had been all over the world as a traveling journalist, and he was well into his forties with a bit of fame of his own by the time he made it to Argentina. But what Carpenter saw turned him into a gushing adolescent, and it was no wonder.

Buenos Aires had come a long way from the days of canceling operas because of rain. The cowboy town of just two decades before had largely vanished. Kerosene and horse dung were still the city's dominant smells, but the gauchos were gone and the first automobiles had appeared, beginning a long tradition of chaos on the streets. The American missionary G. Whitfield Ray, who had first visited Buenos Aires in 1889 on his way out to mingle with the gauchos, saw that his dream of civilization had been realized on a return visit barely two decades later: "The streets, as I first saw them, were roughly cobbled. Now they are asphalt paved, and made into beautiful avenues, such as would grace any capital of the world. . . . On those streets the equestrian milkman is no longer seen. Beautiful sanitary white-tiled tambos, where pure milk and butter are sold, have taken his place. The old has been transformed and *progress* is written everywhere."

This great leap forward had been achieved virtually overnight, and with barely any hard work at all. The spread of commercial agriculture—plus the invention of the *frigorífico*, which allowed increasingly sought-after Argentine steak to be chilled and shipped across the Atlantic—was enough on its own to make the country fabulously wealthy. If you had land in Argentina, you had money; soy, wheat, and corn were the surest path to fortune. The Argentine military heroes of a generation previous had hit it big. Just 2 percent of landholders possessed 55 percent of the farmland in Argentina; put another way, scarcely 1,800 people—about enough to fill the Teatro Colón—held an area equivalent to that of Holland, Belgium, and Switzerland combined. These "Lords of the Pampa" were the oil sheiks of yesteryear, with silos instead of wells. They led lives of unthinkable opulence and ease, spending their weekday afternoons at the racetrack, at the café, or in their porteño mansions—everywhere, it seemed, but on the farm. Fully half of *estancias* in Argentina were farmed by someone other than their tenants. Some owners never even set foot in Argentina, preferring to manage their holdings from Paris. "Seldom has Nature lavished gifts upon a people with a more bountiful land," wrote Bryce. But he added, talking of the wealthy, land-owning class: "He is seldom a hard worker, for it has been his ill fortune to be able to get by sitting still what others have had to work for."

The landowners had little time for such laments, and before long the country had given an all-new meaning to the phrase *nouveau riche*. Argentina proved woefully unable to spend its newfound money fast enough. At first the sheiks tried to be responsible; during this era, rather forward-thinking investments were made in schools, roads, subways, sewers, and other accoutrements of a modern country—and yet there always seemed to be piles and piles of cash left over. There are still monuments and structures all over Buenos Aires that reveal just how indiscriminately Argentines of that era sought to unload money, as if they as a nation were simply bored with their fortune. There is one building in particular, a grand, imposing, four-story building with Gothic architecture on Avenida Cordoba that appears at first glance to be a city hall or an art museum. It is covered from top to bottom with marvelous red, green, and yellow porcelain tiles imported from England, and it cost as much to build as the Library of Congress in Washington, D.C. "The houses of rich millionaires in New York have no finer tiles about their mantels than the material which adorns the outside of this building," Carpenter gushed. The building sits on the highest point in the city (although you'd never know, of course, since this is only about three feet higher than anywhere else) and is possibly the most ornately detailed building in all of Buenos Aires. Its purpose? It was, and is, nothing more than an absolutely fabulous water treatment plant, owned today by a company called Aguas Argentinas (itself a subsidiary of a French corporation, despite what porteño taxi drivers may say). The tiled walls are mere facades that cover the twelve iron drums that purify the city's drinking water. Even Carpenter could hardly believe this. "I have seen the tiled walls and roofs of the palaces of the Emperor at Peking," he wrote, "but the water-works building at Buenos Aires has a finer covering."

With regard to the Aguas Argentinas building, Carpenter also noted, forebodingly: "It is said that there was corruption in the letting of the contract for this building, and that the government officials who secured it were able to put in the neighborhood of $1,000,000 into their own pockets." If this made anyone angry, Carpenter did not say. But with so much money flying around, who was going to notice a million missing here and there?

The monuments and kickbacks weren't enough to empty the coffers, so Argentines simply had no choice but to develop a taste for the good life—cost be damned. Being stuck at the end of the world was no longer an obstacle. Argentines imported absolutely everything: their wine, their cigarettes, their literature, their art. Nothing was made at home—why bother? Burton Holmes marveled at this penchant for all things foreign while on a trip to Buenos Aires during this same era. Holmes complained that everything— "even pajamas"—cost twice as much as in New York. For him, the last straw came when he bought a pound of chocolates from a porteño shopkeeper, then returned to complain that they had gone stale.

"Of course señor, they are not fresh," the shopkeeper told him, matter-of-factly. "They are from Paris."

"Why not make fresh ones here?" Holmes inquired.

"No one would buy them, señor, unless they came from Paris."

Argentina was importing its people, too, and, as with everything else, most of the stock came from Europe. Argentina's population nearly doubled, from 3.9 million in 1895 to 7.5 million in 1912. The government actively recruited prospective immigrants in Europe—concentrating its efforts particularly on countries like France, Holland, and England, hoping they would help make Argentina "whiter," in accordance with the prejudices of the times. The official incentives for new arrivals were documented by a somewhat jealous-sounding correspondent for *Time* magazine: "Instead of maintaining a dread, jail-like Ellis Island, the government at Buenos Aires welcomes immigrants in a spotless hotel, transports them to wherever they decide to settle, and both feeds and lodges them at the destination for a period of ten days."

Despite these efforts, and to the eternal disappointment of the Argentine elite, about half of the new arrivals turned out to be Italians—and not even the "good kind" from the north, but mostly from the poorer southern regions and Sicily. By the 1910s, it was said there were more pizzerias in Buenos Aires than in Naples and Rome combined. Presumably, it was during this era that Argentine Spanish acquired the Italian lilt that endures to this day. The Italians also seem to have been responsible for the Argentine ritual of male friends greeting each other with a quick kiss on the cheek—which is done nowhere else in the Americas except, possibly, for parts of New Jersey (at least if Tony Soprano is any indication). This era also gave birth to *lunfardo*—the slang language that would soon be incorporated into the tango, which in most cases is simply a hybrid of Italian and Spanish. Italian words like *vento* (literally "wind," but "money" in slang) and *piantar* (to slip away) would make their way into the daily vernacular—and the tango as well. A century later, this legacy endures: One night at a movie theater, an advertisement was played for an Italian restaurant; the entire ad was in Italian. By the end, the theater was roaring with laughter. I turned, bewildered, to my Argentine friend. "Aw, everybody here has a *nona italiana*," he said. "We all understand Italian, even if we don't speak a word."

Other immigrant groups made their own distinct contribution. A visiting French journalist named Alberto Londres wrote: "Steel work, machinery, and the soldiers' pointed helmets are German. Railways, clothes, and tins of mustard are English. Motor-cars, razors, and second-rate education are from North America, the café waiter is Italian, the restaurant waiter Spanish, the window cleaner Syrian." Jews immigrated en masse—Buenos Aires still has the world's seventh-largest Jewish population, easily the biggest in Latin America. Everybody seemed to be speaking their own language. Londres described the city as "Babel multiplied a thousand times." This was symptomatic of an odd (and enduring) Argentine truth: nobody seemed interested in fully integrating. It can be said that immigrants to the United States usually became "American," at least within a generation. In Argentina, by contrast, the new arrivals invariably referred to themselves as French or Italian, even if they had lived in Argentina for thirty years. It seems that if Europeans went to the United States to start a new life, they came to Argentina to get rich, and nothing more. They stuck to their old languages, kept their old customs, and usually harbored grand dreams of returning to Europe once they made their fortune.

That said, of all the foreign communities in Argentina, perhaps none took to their new home quite as enthusiastically as the British. The lure of the gauchos might have kept them from conquering Buenos Aires with troops a century earlier, but they came armed with money, and they returned to run what was, at least in economic terms, an unofficial outpost of the British Empire. The *anglo-argentinos* provided the financing and the know-how for nearly every aspect of Argentina's awesome exporting machine, from the giant refrigerated boats to the construction of the ports, the steam engines, and the railroad ties themselves. Nearly two-thirds of Argentina's foreign investment came from Britain, which was rapidly industrializing and therefore increasingly reliant upon Argentine beef, wheat, and other raw commodities; in modern terms, you could say that the English countryside had been outsourced to Argentina. The *anglos* made themselves thoroughly comfortable in Argentina and were almost as influential as the Italians in forging the country's new identity: Soccer was played for the first time in Argentina at the English High School; the Buenos Aires Cricket Club drew large crowds; rugby became popular as well. An Englishman named Brown helped start the Argentine Navy, and Harrods, the venerable British department store, chose to open up an outlet on Calle Florida long before even considering one in the United States. Even today, if you bump into a porteño, he is just as likely to say "*sori*" as "*disculpá.*" In Buenos Aires apartments, a dining room is called *el living;* the mall is *el shopping;* and a dinner jacket is *el smoking.* This degree of cultural assimilation stunned the author Phillip Guedalla, who was particularly struck by the *Buenos Aires Herald,* one of two English-language daily newspapers that contained detailed lists of outgoing ships and grain prices: "They serve an English world that moves sedately up and down between the office and its garden in the outskirts, taking lunch at the English Club or at Harrods, where the southern skies look down upon a splendid replica of Brompton Road. . . . For Argentina is, perhaps, the one foreign country in the world where England has made herself thoroughly at home."

Whatever their nationality, those new arrivals lucky enough to have either land or a bit of starter capital were soon able to revel in their wealth, infected by the optimism that seemed to blow in with every fertile breeze from the Pampas. The architectural style of the times was a chaotic melting pot—Renaissance, gothic, Rococo, and neoclassic—a mix described by one visitor as "progressive euphoria." It was as if Argentina was invincible. Even if the politics were a bit shaky, there was a feeling that Argentina's natural gifts—namely, several feet of black topsoil—would cure all. "God fixes by night what Argentines ruin during the day," went a popular expression. "Nature here embellishes so rapidly with its foliage and its flowers," wrote Carpenter, "that sordidness and abandoned spots never prevail." Burton Holmes went as far as to venture: "There are no beggars left to parade their prosperous poverty through the streets of the great city." This was a gross error in observation, but a telling one.

Amid all the gold-plated mansions and shiny new cars, one thing in Argentina truly screamed wealth and status, for in those years of plenty, there was only one commodity that was truly scarce—and that was women. Due to the nature of immigration, there was a perpetual imbalance between the genders in Argentina. In Buenos Aires in 1910, there were 100,000 more males than females, out of a population of about 1.5 million. "Men, nothing but men," Alberto Londres wrote. On Sundays and Thursdays, the rich went cruising in Palermo Park; their silver and gold-plated carriages might have gone unnoticed, but if they had beautiful girls riding along with them, heads turned. The ladies were a parade of diamonds, rubies, emeralds, sapphires, opals, and gold, of course, gold galore. At the race track—where a seat at the grandstand cost as much as a horse on the Pampa, about ten pesos—no one of class would dare visit without a dame on his arm.

Nowhere was this display more prevalent than at that grand center of belle époque porteño culture, the Teatro

Colón. Built in 1908 and widely acknowledged as one of the finest opera houses in the world alongside Paris and Vienna, it was blessed by marvelous acoustics and an ornate exterior that glimmered like a beacon when lit up at night. The Colón was "no ordinary South-American opera house," *Time* magazine sniffed, "such a dirty and pretentious little place as is to be found in almost every town, full of onion-eating opera lovers gazing at tenors who yodel and choke." Since the southern opera season occurred during the lulls in the North American and European calendar, the Colón was often able to attract the finest European talent. Every Saturday night, it played host to the country's richest landowners, who came to watch the opera—but mostly each other. (The anarchists thought to bomb the Colón as early as 1910, long before they honed in on the La Biela café.) Then as now, the Colón served one real purpose; one writer described the place as nothing more than "a marriage fair." Georges Clemenceau thought it the world's best opera house, but he too focused on what was really important: "the seats peopled by young women in gala dress, the most brilliant spectacle I have ever seen inside a theatre."

Here, the rich had their most intolerable monopoly. From the outside looking in, for those lonely, newly arrived souls who had no women of their own, it must have been absolute torture.

I CAUGHT A GLIMPSE OF WHAT ARGENTINA COULD HAVE been—should have been—one night at the Colón during a performance by the internationally renowned pianist Daniel Barenboim. It was one of my first assignments as a reporter. Barenboim was a bit out of the Colón's league by this time; he was the director of orchestras in both Berlin and Chicago, and he had achieved some notoriety in the film *Hilary and Jackie*, which had portrayed his marriage to the late cellist Jacqueline du Pre. He had made countless recordings and played to packed music halls all over the world. People of Barenboim's acumen simply didn't play in Buenos Aires anymore; yet, in what seemed almost like an accident of history, Barenboim was in fact Argentine. He had played his first public recital in Buenos Aires at the age of seven. Like so many native sons, Barenboim had found true success only after leaving the country—his family had moved to Israel just a few years after his debut—but now, in an almost unprecedented gesture, he was returning to his birthplace to commemorate the fiftieth anniversary of that first performance.

The Colón was electric that night; it was as if Argentina was *important* again, vibrant and alive with a rare sense of pride. Wealthy old members of the elite—people who seemingly hadn't ventured beyond their Recoleta apartments in twenty years—gathered to celebrate the country's momentary return to the world stage. For a night, at least, Argentina could pretend it was on a par with Europe, with the homeland. When Barenboim walked out on stage to address the crowd, the entire theater became respectfully silent.

"I toyed around with the idea of playing the same program as the one I did fifty years ago," Barenboim began, "but I was afraid. I was afraid there would be people here with good memories, and they wouldn't like it as much!"

The crowd went wild with applause. People seemed thrilled less by the substance of Barenboim's speech than by the delivery—after half a century outside Buenos Aires, he still spoke with an unmistakable porteño accent.

From there, though, things went slowly, horribly awry in a way that was only possible in Argentina. Many in the crowd began coughing uncontrollably, a wet, chronic hack, like the Colón had suddenly been transformed into one giant tuberculosis ward. To the porteño elite, this was the distinct, grating sound of the Third World, an unwelcome reminder of what Argentina really was. The well-dressed began furiously reprimanding the offenders, to the point that every break between songs was a cacophony of coughs and shushes. Barenboim appeared singularly irritated. This was not the refined crowd he remembered from 1950, when after seven encores he had to apologize to the crowd and stop playing because his repertoire had been exhausted. Perhaps overcome by nostalgia (maybe Barenboim was in touch with his Argentine side after all), he had decided, apparently ahead of time, that on this night, damn the consequences, he would play *nine* encores. Yet here the masses' enthusiasm waned for a man who, after all, had been gone for many years, and by the third encore almost the entire audience had departed. Barenboim began playing a half-hearted tango, and still the exodus did not stop. Barenboim stubbornly soldiered on, but even from the box seats I could see him turning a bright red, furiously reaching the same conclusion as the tsk-tsking elite: Argentina is a fraud, these people don't appreciate me, and I can't believe I condescended to play for these goddamn *indios*.

When the show finally came to its merciful end, I went backstage. There was yelling and screaming from behind the dressing room door, which was not exactly soundproof. "It went badly," his publicist explained to me. "Give him just a moment." When the door swung open, we briefly made eye contact, and the moment it closed Barenboim began bellowing anew: "I won't do it! I won't do it! Reuters sent a *boy*! I'm not doing the interview! They sent a child!"

An hour later, after much cajoling, Barenboim sulked into a red cushioned chair in one of the box seats and unhappily began: "This country was rich, you know. . . . "

BUENOS AIRES HAD BECOME A CITY OF LINES. AT BANKS, people waited for hours, nervously checking their watches, pleading with the sun as it receded behind the mirrored buildings of the *microcentro*. Some customers camped out on lawn chairs, drinking maté tea and chain-smoking. Others munched on little *miga* sandwiches that the banks were handing out, gratis, hoping to avert—or, in retrospect, at least postpone—an outright revolt.

The lucky ones made it inside the bank before closing time. Upon reaching the teller window, they smiled grimly, presented their withdrawal slip and all recited the same line: "*Dame todo*"—"Give me everything," like it was some kind of hold-up. And in a sense, it was. Entire life savings were quickly counted out in $100 bills—U.S. dollars, at least for the moment—and handed over in a crisp white envelope. Before venturing back out to the street, people stuffed the money inside their clothes. Men carefully stashed a few wads of cash in each pocket, hedging their bets; women typically put the entire sum down the front of their shirt; the rich brought duffle bags. Before long, the slow bleeding had turned into a gush, and $1 billion a day was flowing out of Argentine banks.

At the embassies, the lines stretched even longer, sometimes for blocks. Here, people waited to apply for a passport so they could leave Argentina forever—and return to the homeland of their grandparents, completing a century-long circle that was uniquely Argentine in its own bitter way. Here, sleeping bags and tents were the rule. On nearby telephone poles, gifted entrepreneurs hung makeshift cardboard signs that said "*Hago cola*," or "I'll stand in line for you," with a cell phone number listed below. Those people made a small fortune, but seemingly everybody else was broke and heading to the airport. Every evening outside the departure area at Ezeiza Airport, a large crowd of bleary-eyed families gathered to say good-bye to the people—inevitably young, well-educated twentysomethings—who were boarding the overnight flights to Madrid, Milan, or Miami.

Being in Argentina was like watching a beautiful old mansion crumble brick by brick. At the entrance of one of Buenos Aires' rapidly growing shantytowns, a cardboard sign read "Welcome, middle class!" More *cartoneros* seemed to appear each night in the streets, their cardboard in tow. Argentina had become a global synonym for mismanagement and corruption; some would later call it the Enron of countries. Pawn shops did a brisk business; people sold the family diamonds or even their own hair to make a little cash. Hard currency was hard to come by; many of the country's twenty-three provinces had run out of cash to pay government workers, so they had begun issuing their own currency: For an American equivalent, this was like Texas or Mississippi suddenly deciding to produce their own money. Entre Rios province issued the *federal*; Buenos Aires the *patacon*; La Rioja, the much more prosaic *evita*. At some impromptu markets, the concept of money vanished altogether; people resorted instead to *trueque*, the barter system, trading haircuts for potatoes, palm readings for a kilo of beef. The Argentine economy was now back in the Stone Age.

Nobody really knew where to direct their rage. President De la Rúa made for a lousy villain—how could you hate a guy in an ascot? Aloof, distant, and thoroughly disinterested in the exercise of power, De la Rúa was perhaps most famous for the outcome of his plan to switch Argentina to Daylight Savings Time. Several congressmen had cried conspiracy, protesting that pushing the clocks ahead by an hour during summer would benefit the energy companies—never mind that the opposite was true—and De la Rúa, true to form, had backed down under pressure. After that episode, nobody could take the old man seriously. He had seemed most at ease in his previous career, hosting a call-in radio show for pensioners. "He would make an excellent prime minister of Switzerland," his spokesman once said; being president of Argentina, though, seemed to bewilder him. He once told his cabinet that he would rather be running Argentina's national parks. As the crisis became worse, he retreated for days at a time, stopped talking to the press, and mumbled at public appearances. Rumors swirled that either he was an alcoholic or he had suffered a stroke. Several congressmen publicly accused him of being autistic. On *VideoMatch*, the country's most watched television show, a truer-than-life impersonator portrayed De la Rúa pleading with a cow, desperately trying to get it to milk itself.

Without an obvious scapegoat, Argentines were left to engage in deep soul-searching. The bestseller list was dominated by books with titles like *The Argentine Mystery*, *Who Are We?*, *Requiem for a Lost Country*, *Don't Be Afraid*, *Leaving*, and *Nobody Leave without Giving Me My Money Back*. Perhaps most popular was a book called *El Pelotudo Argentino* (*The Argentine Jackass*), which had a shiny mirror on the front cover.

It was impossible to overestimate the degree to which the crisis dominated all conversations in Argentina, from the café con leche at the family breakfast table to the office coffee machine to the midnight espresso. Whereas stable countries tended to run mindless situation comedies on television during the prime-time evening hours, Argentine airwaves served up a homogenous diet of nail-biting news and public affairs programs. It was all crisis, all the time. During one period of burnout, I invented what I called the Five Minute Challenge. The goal was to talk with an Argentine—friend or stranger—for more than five minutes without the crisis coming up. It was impossible. One time, in a taxi cab, I managed to steer clear of the subject for a full four and a half minutes by babbling on relentlessly about the weather. I was thirty seconds away from triumph when I was torpedoed:

ME (pointing toward the horizon): "Looks like some storm
    clouds gathering over there."
TAXI DRIVER: "Yes. But nothing compared to the storm clouds
    gathering over the economy!"

I didn't talk to any taxi drivers for a month after that. There seemed to be only one place where I could truly escape.

MARIELA SPENT MOST OF OUR SECOND CLASS JUST TRYING to get me to slow down.

"You can stop to take pauses," she explained patiently. We were holding each other in the middle of the dance floor, our feet still grazing each other in midstep, but she had held her head away from me, taking a certain distance so she could be sure she was getting her message across. Her slender neck was exposed. "The tango allows for these pauses. Other dances, like the salsa, I pause and, hmm, I've made a mistake. But here it's intentional. The tango has natural *rupturas* in the music where you can take a little rest. Listen."

This seemed far-fetched. The tango playing on the radio was fast-paced, frantic, like hyperventilation set to music.

"Give it a try," she said.

I pulled her back in, flared out my right hand, and we resumed lurching madly about. I tried to time pauses to the music, but there was just no way to know what was coming next. Tango defied the verse-chorus-verse-chorus-bridge-chorus formula of pop music that had been ingrained in my mind by too much Radio Horizonte in my kitchen. Every time I managed to bring a step to a somewhat dignified halt, the piano went on some mad staccato rampage, as if to taunt me. I stood still, foolishly, for a few moments, surrendered to the ongoing noise, and weakly commenced moving again. I was on the verge of letting loose a frustrated primal scream when suddenly Daniel materialized, like a ghost, right there in front of us.

His eyes were eager, searching, and infused with that same annoying, perky optimism I had seen in the first class. "How's he doing?"

She smiled at me with heartbreaking sympathy. "He's trying," she said. "Still very unsure of himself."

"Has his posture improved?"

"Not yet. It's just the second class. . . . "

"Is there any hope for him using the traditional approach?"

"Maybe."

They eyed me skeptically, like two veterinarians deciding whether to euthanize a sick dog.

"Let me watch you," Daniel declared, his eyes finally settling on me. "I'll see if I can define the problem."

Who the hell was this guy, anyway? What was his role here? Was he merely the diagnostician, charged with dispensing words of vague advice? Was he getting half the cut for this bullshit? A 10 percent finders' fee? Mariela seemed to be doing all the hard work. That morning, the student prior to me had been female, a soulless Russian woman named Svetlana with a silver hoop nose ring, yet even then the arrangement was similar, with Mariela dancing the part of the male—leading—while Daniel was nowhere to be found, presumably lounging about in his boxers upstairs, counting his money.

Daniel folded his arms expectantly.

I stepped close to her—though not quite as close as before—and embarked on step one of the dreaded seven-step sequence.

"*Incorrecto*!" he barked.

Mariela broke our embrace and took a large stride away from me. Her shoulders slumped in defeat. She seemed to be taking all this much harder than I was.

Daniel smiled in apology. "I hope I'm not being too tough," he said, "but if you learn bad form now, you'll never recover. We have to do everything correctly, *bien prolijo*, from the very beginning. Mariela, come stand in front of me."

She obeyed.

He took her into his arms. "The most important part of dancing is the embrace. If the embrace is wrong, then your range of motion will be limited, and you won't be able to take the right steps. More important, you won't be able to seduce the woman! And that's what's important, *no*?" He chortled, insincerely and a bit nervously, I thought, at his own joke. "Your pectoral muscle has to line up here," he continued, pointing to Mariela's sternum. And then, to emphasize his point, he hit the area with a karate choplike gesture, right between her breasts.

"You have to be right *here*," Daniel said, chopping the same spot yet again. This time, she winced. "If you're not lined up correctly, the whole axis is thrown off, and then you won't be able to. . . . "

Daniel kept on yammering, but my attention was now fully devoted to Mariela, and the look of unconcealed resentment that had appeared on her face. As he led her, dancing around the room, continuing to drone on about her axis and his, she stared straight ahead, inert, like a mannequin.

". . . learn good habits now, and then we can teach you more complicated things." They stopped moving now, and, hand on hips, he turned to Mariela. "Maybe you should just have him walk by himself."

"I don't want to walk by myself," I declared, surprised by how resolute I sounded. "I can do that at home. That's not why I'm here."

Mariela smiled with apparent relief.

Daniel froze, speechless, obviously unaccustomed to contradiction. All the poise and good humor had drained out of him in one blow. His impeccable posture went abruptly limp. I realized that I had embarrassed him in front of his— what was she, exactly?—and now, to my surprise, I felt sorry for him. The whole arrangement must have been torture for Daniel. His business basically depended on Mariela being attractive, on her tantalizing her defenseless male customers with at least a hint of sex. Hounds like me spent hours at a time embracing her, trying to seduce her, desperate to decipher whether the electricity in the room was real or just an act coldly conceived to extract the fee of twenty pesos per hour. I found myself marveling at the whole situation. I had signed up for a simple dance lesson, yet here I was, having to delicately negotiate the egos of two people, their manias, my relationship with each of them, and God knows what else, all in their own house. Only the tango, I thought. Did Gardel have to deal with this kind of drama? Was this what he was singing about?

Daniel muttered something inaudible, smiled, then slowly pivoted and walked gracefully out of the room.

"You'll have to excuse him," she said, uncertainly, after he had gone. "*Es un hombre gentil. . . .* He is a kind man, but on occasion he lets his passion"—that word again—"overcome him. He cares too much, sometimes."

"Besides, I think you have a nice embrace," she continued, a soft smile returning to her face. "I think that, with you, it's a question of intention. You seem lost, like you don't know what you'll do next. It's like if you get into a car. If you have no idea where you're going, then it's not probable that you'll arrive well."

With this, something clicked. If I could start thinking four or five steps ahead, rather than just panicking in the moment, then my steps would presumably be firmer, and the intention clearer. And if knowing how to lead was truly the essence of the tango, as El Tigre had told me, then the other problems might solve themselves.

Feeling we might be on the verge of a breakthrough, I nodded and signaled her to come closer. She complied, staring intently at my face, as if sensing my confidence. I took her by the hand and visualized, ahead of me and to the left, what the steps would look like. I was still thinking of the steps mathematically—1, 2, 3, 4, 5, 6, 7—but I now had a preconceived wrinkle thrown in. Between steps 5 and 6, just as the piano went silent and gave way to a violin solo, I shifted my weight and. . . .

"*Ay*," she sighed happily. "What a nice pause!"

I finished the sequence. On the next loop, I cleanly executed the 7–3 step that she had taught me in the first lesson, followed by yet another pause.

She pulled her head back and beamed at me, utterly radiant. "You see, Brian? Maybe you're not a lost cause after all!" Then she leaned back in, pressed her cool cheek against mine and sighed.

THE WAITER BROUGHT US RAVIOLI WITH RICOTTA ON A SIL-
ver plate. I ate and sipped my beer in silence for a good half-
hour before turning to El Nene:

"I think I'm in love with my tango teacher."

He smiled grimly. "You're fucked."

"It's a cliché, isn't it?"

"I don't know," El Nene sighed. He stopped himself. "Well,
yes. It is clearly a cliché to fall in love with your tango
teacher. They've already made numerous movies about this.
Go rent one at Blockbuster, take it home, and jerk off to it.
It'll make you feel better. Seriously. What do you want me to
tell you?" He laughed, his face glowing orange in the candle-
light. "But it's natural, *Che*: This dance, it's impossible to
avoid this sort of thing. You're in this intimate embrace,
holding someone for hours at a time. This person is teaching
you, trying to help you find something deep down inside
you. Because," he continued, scooting his chair closer and
leaning his elbow confidentially on my shoulder, "a good
tango teacher, an authentically good tango teacher, isn't
teaching you steps. She's teaching you to *feel* what the tango
is, and that means feeling a different way about yourself. So
fall in love, *Che*. It's okay. You'll end up being a better dancer
in the end. Just don't let the jealous boyfriend catch you
fucking."

SOME NOT-SO-SUBTLE HINTS AS TO THE TANGO'S ORIGINS
can be found in the titles of some of the earliest songs: "Siete

pulgadas" ("Seven Inches"), "Dos sin sacar" ("Twice without Pulling Out"), "Soy tremendo" ("I Am Tremendous"), and the rather less metaphorical "Cachucha pelada" ("Bald Pussy"), among others.

The world that gave rise to this music was separate, though never far removed, from the belle époque bonanza on the other side of town. Even Frank G. Carpenter, he of the honey-lipped heiresses, noticed there was a different reality beyond the walls of the Teatro Colón. "There is low life as well as high life in the Argentine Republic," Carpenter grudgingly admitted. "The poor are in the majority."

From the beginning, there was a particularly intense resentment among the poor in Buenos Aires, the kind of fury borne from the proximity of inaccessible, extreme wealth. They could smell the Pampa in the air, and they could see the wealth beneath their feet: nine feet of black topsoil, sitting there, waiting to be tilled. But in practice, that was as close as they got. Instead of fanning out to the countryside, like immigrants did in the United States, new arrivals usually found themselves marooned in Buenos Aires, a city of tremendous riches, all of them beyond their reach. Had they crossed an ocean for this? Kashimir Edschmid, a German who approached Buenos Aires by boat, recorded: "There was something horrifying about it, something crushingly cruel about the way in which the inhuman wealth of the city was bound to impress the immigrants as they crawled from the bowels of the ships. Immigrants without money? They were bound to be crushed by the sight of Buenos Aires."

It is estimated that nearly half of the immigrants returned to Europe; those who stayed often did so not out of conviction but because they didn't have the return fare. They were shipwrecked, poor, and generally unafraid of making their displeasure known. In the summer of 1910, a bomb exploded in the Colón. In a separate incident, a porteño chief of police was killed by a bomb thrown by a Russian anarchist. Indeed, anarchism was particularly prominent among the migrant workers from southern Italy and Spain. Argentina also had certain qualities that made it appeal to another, less savory kind of immigrant—it was distant, thinly populated, comfortable, and the rule of law was not exactly pervasive. As an added bonus, it had no extradition treaty. "Criminals from everywhere have taken advantage of this," Carpenter wrote, "and it is said that Buenos Aires has more men living under assumed names than any city in the world." A great many American outlaws were living in the city, among them Butch Cassidy and the Sundance Kid, who passed through Buenos Aires on their way to Patagonia in 1901.

Many of the new immigrants lived in mansions that had once been occupied by the city's richest families; that was as close to the wealth as they got. The mansions had been abandoned during the yellow fever epidemic that swept Buenos Aires during the 1870s, when everybody who could afford to do so fled to higher ground in the new neighborhoods of Barrio Norte and Palermo. In their new incarnation, each room in the mansion housed an entire family, with dozens of families often packed into a single decaying house. It was estimated that four-fifths of working class families lived in one-room households. The arrangement was known as a *conventillo*. With its open common areas and uncomfortably close quarters, it would become like a Petri dish for the development of the tango.

In between visits to the Jockey Club and the Rosedal, Carpenter found time to visit a *conventillo*:

> It received but little sun, and there was a damp, green mold on the stones not trodden by the tenants' feet. Just outside each room in the court was a bowl of charcoal which served as the cook-stove of the family within. Upon some of the fires rested pots of steaming soup, with ragged Italian women bending over them. In one doorway, there was a portly, gray-haired Indian dame cleaning a cabbage, and next to her a lean Spanish woman cooking macaroni. . . . Many rooms have only one bed, which is occupied by the parents and as many children as can crowd in; the remainder of the family must sleep on the floor. There is no way of heating the rooms. They were all dirty and more like caves than the homes of human beings.

It was a threadbare, bleak existence. While life might not have been quite as miserable as Carpenter portrayed it—an enduring Argentine saying holds that even the poorest immigrant could afford his daily steak—there was one essential reality that pushed many *conventillo* dwellers over the edge. Indeed, among the new arrivals, nothing caused as much resentment or fury as the utter lack of women in Argentina, reputable or otherwise. All the girls seemed to be at the Colón, or riding along in the little carriages on Sunday in the park. Starting in this era, and for many decades afterward, the seeming inability of an honest man of modest means to find a suitable mate would be seen as a representation of everything that was wrong and unjust in Argentine society.

In the meantime, if they wanted companionship, or a little something more, there was usually only one option available.

Indeed, by the turn of the century, Buenos Aires was probably home to more prostitutes than any other city in the world, according to the Argentine historian Andres M. Carretero. Most of the working-class brothels were concentrated along Calle Defensa, today the main tourist axis of San Telmo (most modern-day guidebooks are loathe to mention this). There were a few Indians among the prostitutes; many of them had been captured during the Desert Campaign and sold into slavery. But most of the brothel workers came from abroad. Forget Burton Holmes' little chocolates from Paris; girls were Argentina's most coveted import. The most sought-after women were from France; they cost five pesos (a Pole cost only two), and for years the opening line used by all prostitutes at porteño brothels was "I'm from Paris, you know"—the "This is my first night working here" of its day— no matter how distant either line was from the truth. Over time, the lunfardo term *"franchucha"* came to be used interchangeably to mean a French woman or a prostitute. Meanwhile, for reasons unknown, the managers of the brothels were usually Slavs. Women also hailed from Germany, Italy, Ukraine, and, well, pretty much everywhere. During those years, Buenos Aires acquired a reputation throughout Europe as a major center for the trade of sex slaves; it is not hard to understand why.

Yet there was more to the brothels than just sex. They also made a fantastic place to make friends (even the male kind), listen to music, and hear news, rumors, and information about jobs. Even well-to-do Argentine politicians recognized their importance; three Argentine presidents were known to have made campaign stops in brothels (one of them, Leonardo Alem, was even said to have been challenged to a knife fight). As wave after relentless wave of immigrants arrived, the industry expanded at a torrid pace. Brothels increasingly had to compete with cafés, where thinly disguised prostitution was rife. In turn-of-the-century Buenos Aires, even the waitresses were turning tricks. The city's first cafés were violent, bawdy places where an immigrant could pick out a woman, watch a knife duel on the sidewalk outside, listen to some music, and, oh, perhaps drink a coffee or two if the mood hit him.

Faced with such cutthroat competition, brothels had to offer something extra, a kicker. So, they often offered their clientele the opportunity to dance with their women as a way of choosing one. It is easy to imagine the appeal this would have exercised over a newly arrived male immigrant from, say, Italy. Fresh off the boat, he could enter a brothel, meet a woman to his liking, and hold her close, pretending she was his own. Having a couple of dances was certainly more civilized than cutting straight to the deal; not all of these men were animals, after all; many were merely very lonely, suddenly thousands of miles away from those they loved. Maybe, as he danced with her, he thought of his family back home in Naples; maybe he thought of anything but. Generally, after the third song, the client would take the woman to a back room, and complete the transaction.

Over time, no dance would prove to be better suited to this pursuit than the tango. It became the great equalizer, a way to seduce without the interference of money or class. It would become the dance of lonely men everywhere.

Daniel was sitting in the kitchen smoking a cigarette and eating a bowl of raisin bran. That he managed to do both at the same time was not even the unusual part; most Argentines preferred to skip breakfast entirely and opt only for the cigarette.

When he finally looked up and saw me, he smiled.

"Are you enjoying yourself?" he asked.

"What?"

"Are you having a good time with the tango?"

"Well, yes."

"Good," he replied, turning the page on his newspaper. "That's what's important. Have a seat. Mariela will be just a moment. She is with some Vietnamese guy right now. He speaks no English, he speaks no Spanish. Can you believe it? Somehow, she'll manage to *reach* him. She always does. Marvelous girl." He shuffled the paper for a moment, but the pages would not come unstuck in the humidity, so he tossed it on the floor, right next to the ever-present sleeping bag by the TV, and shifted his full attention to me. "So, when did you start learning the tango?"

"A few months ago."

"Ah, so you're new. *Me da envidia.*"

"Why?"

"Because you appreciate the tango for what it is. The tango was taken away from me—forbidden—before I really understood my passion for it."

"Forbidden?"

"You don't understand. You will one day, when you get married. It was like this: I used to go out every night with my friends, dancing tango, going to horse races, playing soccer during the days. I had a job, of course—I was a vegetable deliveryman—and I made decent money, but I liked to have my fun too, *entendés*? First, my wife said no more soccer. She was worried for my knees. I said okay, that's reasonable. After that she said, 'Daniel, we have no money, you can't go anymore to the races.' That was tough, *Che*, that was tough. But I didn't want any problems, so I agreed. *Da da da*, a thousand other things, one by one. Then one night she says to me: 'Daniel, the kids need you at night, you can't go dance tango anymore.'"

He shook his head and took a deep drag off his cigarette. "One day," he sighed, "you wake up, you're forty years old, and you realize you're not yourself anymore. All the things that made you who you are—they're gone. So you. . . . "

The door to the studio flew open, and a tiny Vietnamese man burst into the kitchen, his cheeks flushed bright red.

Daniel stood up from his chair, smiled at the man, and bowed. "Thank you!" he yelled in English. The Vietnamese man did not acknowledge him or even break his stride as he hurried out the door. His eyes were fixed downward, sheer panic telegraphed all over his face. "Thank you! Thank you!" Daniel yelled after him. Daniel started to laugh when he realized the Vietnamese man had gone and was never, ever coming back. "Thank you! *Konichiwa!*"

Mariela came into view through the doorway, doubled over in laughter.

"What did you *do* to him?" Daniel shrieked, happily scandalized.

"I don't know!" she replied, laughing so hard that she had to gasp for breath. "I couldn't understand a word the poor man said! One minute we were dancing, *todo bien,* and the next, he looked like he was about to faint!"

Daniel shook his head in mock pity. "I told you that blouse was too much," he said, pointing at her extremely revealing pink top. "You can't torture the poor foreigners like that! If the poor Vietnamese man had been twenty years older, he might have had a heart attack! You have to be more careful, *querida!*"

Mariela smiled thinly and looked down at the floor, blushing.

"Okay," Daniel said, turning to me. "Well, I guess it's your turn." He winked and clapped a good-natured hand on my back. "Have fun."

I entered the studio, resentful that the enemy had just been humanized.

The door closed and Mariela and I were alone.

"So what *did* happen with *el vietnamés?*" I asked.

She shrugged. "Too much passion, I suppose." She smiled and patted my shoulder, a devious glint in her eye. "Don't worry. For your own good, we'll try to protect you."

By the end of the first tango, though, any pretense of "protecting" me was quickly forgotten. Something different was in the air today. She sighed with delight after each step. "Marvelous, just marvelous," she would whisper, so close I could feel her lips tickle my ear. Her chest grazed mine with each twisting *giro* half-turn, left to right, right to left. I stared at her neck. I felt a scratch in my throat. We danced several songs in silence until she stepped away, folded her arms, and smiled.

"Good," she declared, seemingly amused. "Excellent."

"What?"

Mariela laughed. "You have no idea, do you?"

I shook my head.

"*Regio, el tango que bailaste.* You danced a lovely tango. And I believe that you weren't even thinking about the steps, were you? Your mind was in another place."

My cheeks were flushed.

"This is real progress," she decided, tapping her forehead thoughtfully with her index finger. Then she delicately moved back toward me and whispered: "Listen. I'm going to be at the Confiteria Ideal next Thursday evening, alone. It might be a good opportunity for us to practice further without interference. You understand?"

At that moment, I would have gone with her anywhere. "Yes," I nodded. "Thursday, then."

"*Muy bien, entonces.*" The class was over. She stretched her arms lazily, and a satisfied half-smile crept across her face. "I wonder if Daniel is still awake," she mumbled to herself. She checked her watch. "I wonder if he's upstairs in bed." She showed me to the door, but it was as if I was already gone.

I FLOATED OUTSIDE AS IF IN A DAYDREAM. IT WAS A RAINY Sunday afternoon, and everybody on the street seemed to be walking with the same punch-drunk pace, although I doubted they had just enjoyed the same kind of privileged experience I had. Most porteños were inside watching soccer—Boca was playing somebody irrelevant like Rosario, and even the usual bloodcurdling scream of "gooooooooooal" from a second-floor TV seemed lazy and uninspired. The smell of sizzling steak and sausage wafted out from the alleyways. The sidewalks were dangerously slippery in my new tango shoes, but I felt oddly, suddenly, invincible. On the yellowed wall of a cheap restaurant, someone had written graffiti: THEY PISS ON US AND THEY SAY IT'S RAINING.

The piss was starting to pick up so I ducked into the Mercado de San Telmo, established 1897. Inside, people were selling old records, post cards, and giant slabs of beef—entire cows, stripped of their skin and hanging by hooks from the ceiling. The rain tapped lightly on the cavernous, corrugated tin roof, which descended to corners with grand ornaments like spokes on a bicycle wheel. A few drops of water sneaked through the roof and dribbled through to the floor. At the front of the market, on a table, sat a half-dozen old gramophones. An elderly British couple were stroking the sleek bronze horn, trying—and failing—to feign disinterest as they negotiated a price with its owner.

". . . buy yourself a real antique," the salesman was saying in English, "that I acquired from an old family, *una familia terrateniente*, a landholding family, suffering hard times."

"That's a shame," the old British man mumbled.

"Not for you! For you, it is lucky!" The remark was uniquely Argentine, somehow bitter and jovial at the same time. "Should I put on some music?"

The couple glanced nervously at each other and nodded.

With a regal bow, the salesman produced a record from under the table. "Then it has to be a tango!" he declared, "for my very, very wealthy English friends."

The *bandoneon* echoed through the hall as I perused the other tables. There was a 1938 travel guide to the Middle

East written in French—I wondered how such a book ended up in Argentina, who held on to it for nearly seventy years, and how on earth it would ever find a buyer now. I gingerly opened the book, and it revealed a meticulously stenciled, idyllic illustration of Iraq. Men in flowing white robes were strolling underneath palm trees by a river. "The good life on the Euphrates," the caption extolled.

Continuing on, there was one stall that seemed to only sell Polaroid-sized photos of Carlos Gardel. An adjacent stand offered old records of Gardel's, with Queen and A-ha and Rod Stewart's greatest hits thrown in for good measure. Toward the exit, there was a silver bucket full of old currency notes in massive denominations, long since worthless, testimony to past decades of interminable inflation and economic chaos. The bills were purple, red, green, and gold, of 500 australes, 1,000 pesos, 5,000 nuevos pesos, and so on, seemingly into infinity, all to be had for ten cents apiece.

In other countries, this would have been an antique fair. In Argentina, it was a museum of past failures. Upon thinking this, I shook my head and laughed: What was happening to me? Anything beautiful reminded me of the past. I was deeply nostalgic for an era that I had never known, in a country that was not my own.

A FEW NIGHTS BEFORE WE WERE TO MEET AT THE CONFITERIA Ideal, Mariela and I had moved on to practicing the *barrida*, a step where I was to use the tip of my foot to send her foot sliding across the floor. Done right, it can be one of the most artful, almost dainty steps. *Barrida* means "sweep"—you sweep the other person's foot along the floor. The step was showy and relatively easy—a rare, perfect combination. But while the *barrida* was mechanically uncomplicated (compared to other tango steps, at least), timing it to the rhythm of the music was a different matter altogether. From beginning to end, the step was supposed to take two beats, which was proving far too fast for me. In a vain attempt to move her foot from my right to left, I ended up *barrida*-ing my own left foot, stumbling, and falling face-down on the hardwood floor.

"*La puta!*" she shrieked, her hands on her cheeks. "What have I done?"

I was laughing as I peeled myself off the floor. Once she realized I was okay, she started cracking up, too. It was the same throaty, uninhibited laugh I remembered from that first night I danced with her at the Niño Bien.

With a loud crash, the door to the kitchen flew open. It was Daniel, and he was furious. His head bobbed about furiously as he surveyed the entire room, like he was searching for evidence of a crime. Sweat poured from his forehead. "What's going on in here?" he demanded to know.

Mariela was still laughing. "He's having some problems with the *barrida*," she said, struggling to regain her composure.

"What kind of problems?"

"Every time he does it, he falls on the floor."

The two of us were giggling like adolescents.

Finally, Daniel decided to smile. "I just wanted to make sure everything was okay," he mumbled. "Maybe I can help you with something?"

Mariela suddenly looked very nervous.

"Sure," I said, though I sensed this might help him more than me. "I can't seem to do the *barrida* fast enough."

He looked at me skeptically. "Velocity is never important in the tango," he said, slowly, as if confused. "You must be doing it wrong. I'll show you."

He crossed the room and embraced Mariela. They danced a few warm-up circles, moving to the music in double-time at an urgent speed that I had never seen before in the tango. When the moment came for the *barrida*, something went awry, and their legs got tangled up in the wrong position. Daniel rolled his eyes and clicked his tongue. "Follow my lead!" he seethed. Then they began the whole loop around the room again, like a plane after an aborted landing.

Had Mariela made the error? They were moving far too quickly for me to discern. But wasn't everything that goes wrong in the tango supposed to be the man's fault?

They returned to the same spot, he rotated his shoulders to the left, lined her up perfectly, and . . . down in flames. This time the collision was so bad that Daniel staggered backward, the first and only time I ever saw him lose his balance. She shook her head in exasperation, eyes cast downward. When he recovered, he stomped back over and grabbed her like a toddler. He put his left hand on the small of her back, smashed his right hand flat against her breasts, and violently corrected her posture.

Mariela groaned in pain and muttered something I couldn't quite hear.

"You can sigh later," Daniel said severely. "For now, you will pay attention."

From there, they descended into some kind of diabolical place I've never visited and, from the looks of it, never care to. They spun around the room with blinding speed, hatred etched all over both their faces. My *barrida* was nowhere to be seen—this was entirely about them now. He led her through sequences of mind-blowing complexity. He marked several *ganchos*, the hook where the woman's leg flies backward between the opened legs of the man. Each time, she kicked with all her might, slamming her heel into his shin with a loud *thwap!* Each *gancho* was surely leaving a healthy knot on his leg, yet he kept marking them, over and over, kick after kick.

Through it all, he was hissing into her ear. "What's the matter with you today?" he was saying. "You're a disaster."

I wilted up against the wall, wishing I wasn't there. I had a distinct feeling that I was watching something I wasn't supposed to see.

Finally, they stopped. Daniel turned to me. Would he leave now?

"Okay, now let's see you do it," he said with a cruel smile.

Mariela must have noticed the look on my face, and she took it upon herself to walk over and initiate the embrace. But, of course, I couldn't lead anything. My hands felt like jelly. For some reason, I couldn't even remember the sequence of steps that would set up the *barrida*. The song was about halfway over when I just shrugged and stopped dancing. "I give up," I said.

Daniel was bright red with fury. "You haven't taught him anything yet," he thundered, looking accusingly at Mariela. *"What have you two been doing in here?"*

He stormed out of the room and slammed the door.

Mariela and I were left facing each other, but her eyes stayed fixated on the floor. I desperately wanted to end the class right there, but I also didn't want to make a scene, figuring that would make things worse for her. Without looking her in the eye, I walked over, drew her close to me, and began dancing. Under different circumstances, in such an embrace, I might have felt like trying to comfort her, but this was the furthest thing from my mind. For reasons I still can't quite explain, and that I'm definitely not proud of, at that moment I felt thoroughly disgusted by her. My attention was devoted only to the clock. We tangoed on half-heartedly, silently, through the last few songs.

At 2 P.M. on the dot, we walked through the door out of the salon, and Mariela beat a hasty path straight to the bathroom. I heard the water in the sink start running.

There at the kitchen table sat an Italian man and a Korean girl. The Italian, who had been staying in Daniel and Mariela's spare bedroom for a few weeks, had his laptop out and was showing off his music collection. They were speaking to each other in terrible pidgin Spanish. I was eager to get the hell out of there, but I had to wait to pay Mariela first.

"¿Te gusta musica?" the Italian was saying with a broad smile.

The Korean was confused. "Ah . . . ah! Si, me gusta," she declared, thrilled.

Ten minutes passed. Then Mariela emerged from the bathroom, the epitome of grace and composure. She showed no signs of having been upset. She looked slightly tired, but that was the extent of it. I thought: aha, she is a pro at this.

She casually walked over to the kitchen sink and began doing dishes. The running water drowned out everything.

The only other noise in the room came from the television, which was tuned to the weather report on Crónica. "182 DAYS UNTIL WINTER," the block letters read.

After a while, the Italian turned to her, pointed to his laptop and said, in Spanish:

"Is this a *waltzer*?"

Mariela turned toward him, blinking. "A what?"

"A *waltzer*."

She searched her head, desperately trying to understand. "You mean a waltz?"

"No!" the Italian growled, growing irritated. "A *waltzer*!"

Mariela stared at him. And then, she just lost it. "I'm so sorry," she gasped, sweetly, tears pouring down her cheeks. "I have no idea what you're trying to say."

Bewildered, the Italian averted his eyes, dropped the subject, and went back to meekly tap-tapping on his laptop. Mariela shuddered with sobs, her shoulders hunched over the sink, as she finished washing the plates on the counter.

When she finished cleaning, she wiped her eyes with the dishrag, made eye contact with me for the first time, and motioned for me to walk outside.

She opened one of the double wooden doors to the street, which was hot with sunlight. I leaned against the closed door and it came unhinged.

I turned in close, my face just an inch away from hers. Red streaks stained the pale skin around her eyes. "Are you okay?" I asked softly. "Is everything okay?"

Her head cocked to the side. "What?" she said. "What did you say?"

And in that instant, I lost my nerve. "Never mind," I said. "See you next week."

As I turned away, I saw a faint smile cross her lips. I walked, almost ran down the sidewalk and didn't even consider looking back. It wasn't until I got home that I realized I had forgotten to pay her.

In 1906, AN ARGENTINE FRIGATE CALLED THE SARMIENTO docked in the French port of Marseille, changing the history of tango forever. An exposition of world culture there called for the performance of "big indigenous parties," and the somewhat bewildered Argentine crew decided to oblige their hosts with a performance of the dance that was still relegated to back alleys at home. The tango was immediately denounced as criminal, lascivious, and immoral; in other words, it was an instant sensation. From there, according to the historian Mardo Zalko, it is believed that French cocaine smugglers carried the tango back to Paris, along with a little something to help melt away the inhibitions inherent to such a scandalous dance. In 1910, almost nobody in Paris had ever heard of the tango. By 1913, it was being danced virtually everywhere—and not just by lonely men in the brothels.

Paris was primed for such a fad. French immigration to Argentina had populated both the universities and the brothels of Buenos Aires, while many among the porteño landholding elite had chosen to make their homes on the Left Bank. There was a mutual love affair between the two cities; porteños frequently quipped that "*Buenos Aires es la esposa, Paris es la querida*—Buenos Aires is the wife, Paris is the mistress." There are at least three hundred tangos that pay homage to Paris; somehow the city and the dance matched each other. Meanwhile, Paris was in a free-wheeling mood—it was, after all, the era of the Moulin Rouge—and hungry for something exotic and new. Parisians were thus able to appreciate the tango purely as a dance, rather than a political statement. Plus, as the author Simon Collier noted, the tango "was sufficiently picturesque to cover up the faults of a bad dancer, and dramatic enough to show off a really good one." Whatever the reason, tango became the dance of choice among the middle classes in the City of Lights. Ricardo Guiraldes, a porteño playboy abroad who was instrumental in popularizing the dance, wrote a poem in which he stated: "Half of Paris now rubs against the other half." The Countess Melanie de Pourtales famously asked: "Is one supposed to dance it standing up?"

Paris being Paris, the phenomenon soon spread to other cities and continents. In January 1914, the *New York Times* ran the headline "ALL NEW YORK NOW MADLY WHIRLING IN THE TANGO." So many dance halls sprang up in the French Quarter of New Orleans that a portion of the area was briefly known as the "Tango Belt." Before long, tango received the ultimate validation when it appeared in a Hollywood movie. The first major film with a tango scene was *The Four Horsemen of the Apocalypse* in 1921, in which Rudolph Valentino appeared, rather intriguingly, as a gaucho—albeit in a ludicrous Aztec poncho and Andalusian hat.

That is not to say, of course, that the tango did not run into its usual critics. The Catholic Church of New York was among the first in the United States to voice objections, calling the dance wild and shameless. An American rabbi remarked that the tango "is prejudicial to a sane view of life, to moral responsibility and the performance of duty." The Spanish magazine *La Ilustracion Europea y Americana* spoke of the "indecorous and by all means reproachable 'tango,' a grotesque ensemble of ridiculous contortions and repugnant attitudes, seemingly impossible to execute, or even witness, by someone who at all esteems his personal dignity."

Elsewhere, the inevitable pattern of virulent rejection and popular acceptance played itself out. Somehow, though, the tango always seemed to come out on top. Kaiser Wilhelm II banned his military officers from dancing it in uniform, effectively killing the phenomenon in Germany—until the Kaiser's own son took a liking to it, and the tango promptly conquered the Rhineland with an efficiency that was, well, almost German. Perhaps nowhere was the tango as popular as in Italy, where the tango was reportedly performed in 1914 for Pope Pius X by a stylish young Roman couple. According to an account in the Parisian magazine *L'Illustration*, the Pope was less than impressed. "I understand that you love dancing; it is carnival time, and you are young," Pius X was reported to have said. "But why adopt these barbarian contortions of Negroes and Indians?"

Back in Argentina, the elite watched in horror as their country became associated with the tango in the mind of the rest of the world. Diplomats believed the dance had permanently stained Argentina's fame abroad; it was briefly banned—to no avail, of course—at the Argentine embassy in Paris. The young country with an inferiority complex had been searching for an identity for decades, and now a vulgar dance from the port ended up being its main export? It was intolerable. When the Argentine ambassador in St. Petersburg was presented to Czar Nicholas II in 1913, the czar was simply heard to remark: "Argentina . . ." and then, in a flash of recognition, "Oh yes, the tango!"

In time, of course, the tango won in Argentina as well. The version of the dance that returned home from Europe was a bit more refined, a bit less vulgar, but it was still the tango. The Parisian influence was clear in the names of the tango halls that would proliferate in Buenos Aires over the next decade: the Abbaye, the Montmartre, and the Folies Bergère. Naturally, by the 1920s the upper classes were claiming that the tango had been their idea all along. The first spot in Buenos Aires where it was considered decent for men and women to dance tango together was in the Prado Español, on Quintana Avenue, just a few blocks away from La Biela. But some among the elite would never accept it; they would just have to wait another three decades until they got their chance to snuff it out.

A *LA MIERDA*," El Dandy muttered darkly. "Fuck it. Let's go rob a bank."

"Don't be a fool," El Nene laughed, choosing not to take him seriously. "The money's not there anymore. The government already stole it from the banks. If you want your money back, then let's go knock on the front door of the Casa Rosada. If *that* is your intention," he offered, regally raising his glass, "then, my friend, I will accompany you."

"It's not fair," El Dandy raged, as if he hadn't heard a word. He began scratching his arm compulsively, as if it was on fire.

"They stole from us. So why don't we steal from them? I know a guy. . . . "

"I'm sure you do."

"He has access to some guns. We could call Johnny the Bard. Do you remember him?"

"*Que boludo,*" El Nene sighed, shaking his head.

For once, on this matter, I was tempted to side with El Dandy. A few days before, determined to stop the run on the banks before the financial system completely collapsed, De la Rúa had ordered all bank accounts frozen. The new rules, known prosaically as *el corralito,* or the little corral (a nice nod to gaucho nostalgia), meant that no one could withdraw more than three hundred dollars in cash per week. Everyone in Argentina conducted all transactions in cash—buying an apartment involved showing up with a suitcase (or usually a garbage bag, to be less conspicuous) with $200,000 in cash. Business had been done this way for decades precisely because of fear that the government would step in and confiscate the money. Now that it had happened, every paranoid Argentine who had kept his life savings stashed under his mattress had been proven right. Assholes like me who had kept their money in the bank looked like *pelotudos.* I was suddenly out $2,000.

"They already robbed us first!" El Dandy seethed. "*Durante sesenta años, me fui rompiendo el culo.* I busted my ass for sixty years. I saved my money. When Menem said 'Bring back the money,' I brought back the money. From the mattress to the bank. And now it's gone! I could have spent it on beer, on whores. . . . "

"You did spend it on beer and whores," El Nene said drolly.

"But not all of it!" El Dandy laughed. "I could have had more girls! But it's gone! What did we work for, boys? All those nights in Miami, in Paris?"

"It wasn't so bad," El Chino #1 protested. "We still had love of the tango. . . . "

"Oh, *shut the fuck up*. That's exactly the sort of philosophy that got this whole country into trouble. We sit around here like a bunch of *boludos*, drinking our whiskey. Look, *muchachos*, I recognize that I'm not starving here. There are people dying in this country. I'm fine, I'm lucky. But I'm just asking, when are we going to say 'enough'? When are we going to demand that these corrupt animals stop ripping us off? I tell you, boys, this past Sunday, I had no cash for steak, no money for the *asado*. So it was raviolis instead. But what happens next Sunday?"

"Next Sunday," El Chino #1 said, "it will just be chicken with rice."

"And the week after that, rice with rice."

The table laughed.

"And then?" El Dandy urged them on.

"Dirt with dirt."

"When the dirt runs out?"

"Shit with shit," El Chino #1 replied, giggling like a little girl.

"But they'll steal the shit, too."

"And *that*," El Dandy said gravely, "is when we *all* starve to death. When does it stop? When do we make it stop?"

part four

"SHE BEAUTIFUL"

Nestled among orange groves and cyprus trees in the rolling hills near the Uruguayan border, there is a small city where it would seem that nothing bad could ever happen. Concordia (population 160,000) is perhaps the lushest spot in an unthinkably lush country, a city known throughout Argentina as *la gran estancia*, "the big farm," an infinite expanse of rich soil that produces some of the country's best beef, milk, and cheese. Settled in part by German immigrants at the turn of the century, the flight crew for the tiny airline that serves Concordia still looks like a creepy fantasy of Hitler's—a regiment of strapping, rosy-cheeked, blond boys with bright blue eyes, serving up Diet Cokes and ham-and-cheese *miga* sandwiches. Their ancestors had rigidly planned a city of square blocks and manicured plazas, blessed with a deepwater port on the Río Uruguay that became a major shipping center for beef bound for Britain and beyond. Antoine de Saint-Exupéry crash-landed near Concordia in the 1930s, and it was said that his visit helped inspire *The Little Prince*. He described the area as "an oasis."

By the time I visited, Concordia had become a caricature of all the country's most irrational and bizarre afflictions. One U.S. dollar could buy 40 pounds of the city's famous oranges; yet, at supermarkets, almost all of the oranges for sale were imported from Israel. Concordia had the highest poverty rate in Argentina; 78 percent of the population was unable to properly clothe or feed itself. Yet in the endless shantytowns that surrounded the still-manicured urban core, there was not a single garden to be seen. Every morning, dozens of people gathered at the city dump and waited in an eerily civilized single-file line for trucks to deliver the day's fresh garbage. They rummaged through piles of cigarette butts and shards of broken glass, searching for half-eaten cartons of yogurt or maybe a chicken bone with some meat still hanging on it. Orange peels were considered the biggest delicacy of all.

So it was somehow fitting that Concordia would be the place where the endgame for the Argentine crisis finally began to unfold. Early one morning, a group of men forced their way into one of the large supermarkets on the edge of town and began carrying out bread, meat, and those delicious Israeli oranges. Word spread, and within minutes half the city was gathered outside, pounding on the glass doors. When the police finally arrived, they did nothing to stop them; instead, they helped determine who among the crowd was pregnant, malnourished, or handicapped and facilitated the delivery of food to the neediest.

Word spread quickly. By that afternoon, eerily similar events were unfolding 600 miles away on the outskirts of Mendoza, the arid wine country on the edge of the Andes. Here, the looters took not only food but VCRs, televisions, and air-conditioning units and, one assumes, a prodigious amount of Malbec. Photos would later surface of uniformed police hauling off giant slabs of steak. Another image of a masked man carrying away a Christmas tree would become an Internet sensation—someone added the caption: "Happy holidays from Fernando de la Rúa and family."

Later that week, as the riots crept toward the capital like a slowly spreading cancer, De la Rúa appeared on television, looking as sanguine and overmedicated as ever. But even he must have realized by now that he was in immense trouble, because—this being Argentina—a supermarket riot was, of course, not *just* a supermarket riot. In a country that produced enough food for 300 million people—nearly ten times its actual population—it was the sheer absurdity of such an act that made it so intolerable. In 1989, when inflation had reached 5,000 percent, supermarket riots had forced the resignation of the then-president, Raul Alfonsin. And that crisis was child's play compared to this one.

"That was a long time ago," De la Rúa said with a dismissive wave when asked if he feared meeting a similar fate. "We don't see any reason for these episodes to be magnified beyond their significance. The problem exists, but it shouldn't be a motive for alarm or to speak of a general conflict."

DE LA RÚA IS AUTISTIC, Crónica declared. SECURITY REINFORCED IN BUENOS AIRES.

ENOUGH OF THIS BULLSHIT," THE TAXI DRIVER DECLARED AS I hopped in the car. "Let's have some rain *en serio*. Don't you think? Let's have some real shit. I'm tired of waiting, aren't you?"

A southeasterly wind was whipping through the skyscrapers downtown, blowing leaves and garbage in crazy directions above Avenida Alem like a ticker-tape parade. Teasing drops of rain trickled from the pitch-black late evening sky.

"Armenia 1366," I said, adjusting my tie.

"To dance?" he asked, impressed.

"To dance."

"*Muy bien*," he said, pulling an abrupt, highly illegal U-turn. The taxi nearly hit a streetlight as we roared back toward Avenida Cordoba to head uptown. "I think it's good that people are still going out. Somebody has to go out and enjoy themselves. Somebody still has to have a little cash. There has to be a middle class. I say this not because of virtuous passion for other people. Look at it like this: You're going to spend money now. And that's great. But I ask you this— what good is it to spend money if fifty starving bastards are chasing after you?

"That's why I say we need a good cleansing. The crisis is tough, but it's positive, you know? You tear it all down, and then you do a redistribution of the wealth *como corresponde*. That's what's needed here. Because this is a rich country, don't you see? We were rich here. We could be rich again, if they'd just give the money to the people!"

We spent the rest of the ride in silence. The rain was pouring down by the time we arrived at the Armenian Cultural Center.

"Tell everybody at the milonga that Jorge sends *saludos*," he spat as I climbed out of the car. "Tell them I might come back next year. God and Fernando de la Rúa willing."

I COULD HAVE JUST GONE HOME, OF COURSE. AS THE FIRST riots began to materialize on the outskirts of Buenos Aires, and the pessimism in the city became even more asphyxiating, the phone calls from Mom became ever more frequent: "Come home, you've got a bedroom here whenever you want it." But every time I dared to entertain such a notion, another long night of dancing, drinking, and camaraderie would remind me why I just couldn't leave, not yet. Places like the Niño Bien were like time machines, the last sanctuaries in the country where greatness still survived. The milongas were by no means impervious to the crisis—ever since El Dandy's furious tirade, even the Council of Elders was obsessively plotting their own boozy version of revolution—but those interminable nights reminded all of us why we were putting up with the squalor instead of lining up at Ezeiza airport with everybody else. One morning, as we stumbled out into the pre-dawn silence, the sky a haunting dark blue, El Nene turned to me and said, quietly: "Even when it's bad, there's nowhere in the world better than Argentina."

This belief—that the country was simultaneously doomed and still the most marvelous place imaginable—was uniquely Argentine. I understood now that, whatever the fundamental cause of Argentina's problems might be, it was no longer relevant. The sheer inertia of the crisis, the fact that things had been so bad for so long, was all that mattered. The pessimism wasn't a psychosis, as I had first suspected—it was, in fact, very rational. Several generations of Argentines had lived through nothing but decline. As logical as progress and growth seemed to me as an American, recession and decay was the norm for them. No wonder nobody invested in anything—the economy was always contracting, and governments were always collapsing. Once you were infected with this virus, it was nearly impossible to shake. (Years later, I still can't quite bring myself to buy stocks or real estate, as ridiculous as that sounds.) Unless someone or something could accomplish the Herculean task of convincing the Argentines that their future might be okay, the country would remain locked in a self-fulfilling prophecy of decline.

I couldn't help but wonder, though, what event, or series thereof, could have possibly delivered the blow that sent Argentina reeling. What could have possibly triggered seventy years of decline? The answer, as usual, seemed to reside in the tango.

ENRIQUE SANTOS DISCEPOLO, THE AUTHOR OF "CAMBALACHE" and the man who chronicled Argentina's decay better than anyone else, began his career as a comedian. It didn't quite work out. He also tried his hand, with somewhat more success, as a film actor—in the movies, Discepolo infallibly played the hapless victim, enduring one humiliation after another, stuttering uncontrollably and joking darkly about his fate, almost like an Argentine Woody Allen. He also directed a few films, and he studied briefly to be a teacher as well. But if there was ever anyone who was born and bred to write tangos, it was Discepolo. This was, after all, the man who famously declared that "the tango is a sad thought that you can dance." Thanks in large part to him, this would become true.

Discepolo's life started out on an appropriately tragic note: he lost his father at age five and his mother at nine, and it may very well have been the sadness of an orphan that would later permeate his tangos. Before he died, Discepolo's father did manage to successfully pass off his own baggage on his son: Santo Discepolo was an Italian-born musician who had studied at the royal conservatory of Naples but, upon getting off the boat in Buenos Aires, had to settle for directing the porteño band of police and firemen. It was exactly the sort of humiliating concession that was (and is) so common among those who emigrate to another country, and this disenchantment would later become perhaps the major theme in Enrique Discepolo's work.

The man was prone to mood swings that would make an opera singer blush with shame: supernova-like outbursts of anger and sudden binges of happiness would define his life. Any self-respecting armchair psychoanalyst would deduce that Discepolo must have suffered from acute depression; were he living today, he likely would blow right through Prozac to lithium and end up in electroshock therapy. He was an epically ugly man; his nose appeared to be dripping off his face, and his sunken cheeks looked to have been bashed in by bricks. Discepolo's biographer, Sergio Pujol, described him as "feeble and shy." He spoke in that elliptical, obtuse manner so common among Argentines even today. Discepolo once said: "A tango can be written with one finger, but with the soul; a tango is the intimacy that is hidden and the scream that comes out naked." I have read this quote a hundred times and I don't have the slightest clue what it means.

It is perhaps surprising that, even before he embarked on his unparalleled career as a tango lyricist, Discepolo had lived a rather comfortable, middle-class life. He was typical of his generation in that most prominent tango composers were not pimps and *compadritos*, but relatively well-off bohemians. He was an anarchist who believed in the logic of the *mala vida*—that prostitution, pimping, and crime was the only way to get ahead. That he espoused these beliefs from the comfort of a nice apartment in Buenos Aires does not appear to have hurt his credibility in the slightest. Discepolo was well-versed enough to know the psychology of his core audience; and he knew that it was the tormented, lonely men who were the angriest of all. The historian Daniel James comments that in Discepolo's tangos, "the impossibility of a meaningful relationship between a man and a woman has come to symbolize the impossibility of any social relationship that is not based on greed, egotism, and a total lack of moral scruples in a world based on injustice and deceit."

Discepolo's first well-known tango, "Que vachache," or "What a Mess," was a thinly veiled critique of Argentine president Marcelo T. Alvear. Tango had always been political, of course, but Discepolo took this, as so many things, to an entirely new level. The song preceded "Cambalache" by nearly a decade but contained many of the same themes, and even some of the phrasing was strikingly similar. Like Discepolo's later body of work, "Que vachache" is striking in its sustained despair:

> What's needed is to put away lots of money,
> Sell your soul, raffle away your heart
> Throw away what little decency you have left
> Money, money, and money . . . money yet again
> That way it's possible for you to eat every day

Have friends, a house, a good name . . . whatever you wish.
True love drowned in the soup,
Your belly is queen and money is God.
Throw yourself in the river! Don't struggle with your conscience,
You're a loser who isn't even worth laughing at
Put food on my table, forget about your decency
Money, money, money, I want to live.
How is it my fault if you've led a decent life,
You act like an imbecile, you eat air and you have no bed?
Who gives a shit? Today all standards are dead,
Jesus is worth no more than a thief.

"Que vachache" premiered in 1926 at a theater in Montevideo, Uruguay, and was angrily whistled down by an unforgivably optimistic audience. The world was not yet ready for Enrique Santos Discepolo.

Indeed, the 1920s had been very good to Argentina (and, by extension, to charming little Uruguay as well). The world's economy had largely healed from the damage of World War I—meaning that demand for Argentina's wheat and beef was robust again—and the construction of mansions in Buenos Aires could happily resume. U.S. president Herbert Hoover visited Argentina and, to the delight of the locals, proclaimed it "the world's breadbasket." Although the tide of new arrivals had begun to thin in comparison to the massive armada of immigrant boats of the previous decade, an Italian or a Spaniard could still come to Buenos Aires with reasonable expectations of a better life. Unrest still fermented among the impoverished—those just off the boats, and especially the single and lonely—but for the moment they could entertain at least the fantasy of one day striking it rich. Democracy had been firmly in place for nearly a half-century. Burton Holmes noted—forebodingly, in retrospect—that soldiers would never stage a coup "as long as commerce keeps control of Argentina's destinies—as long as the people are so busy being prosperous that they have no time for squabbly politics." To this, he confidently added: "The Argentine Republic is now too rich, too prosperous, to indulge in those petty squabbles which have marked the career of other South American republics."

Ana Luciana Devis, Discepolo's lifelong companion, commented on the atmosphere of cabarets in the 1920s: "The patrons were all men of leisure—they had never worked. They drank bottle after bottle of champagne and consumed vast quantities of caviar. They were nice, generous, but irresponsible people. It was not unknown for one of them to give a dancer a country house as a present. The nights passed slowly—they didn't have to rush off anywhere. Even love affairs where money changed hands were subject to a lengthy, patient ceremony; from the time the gentlemen approached the *milonguera*, plying her with drinks, four days would often pass before the adventure took place."

The timelessness of this passage is astounding: Devis could have been describing 1925, 1865, or 2005. But it is clear in retrospect that, then as now, this aura of fat and lazy prosperity was only a small part of the Argentine reality. As Devis wrote this, her own husband was penning furious tangos in the next room. The anger and bitterness expressed in tango lyrics were not merely testimony to a bygone era—Argentina was like a tinderbox waiting to catch fire at any moment. The virulent streak of anarchism and class hatred present in Argentine society since the days of the gauchos was readily apparent to anyone who looked closely enough. When Albert Einstein visited Argentina in 1925, he was said to have asked: "How can such a disorganized country progress?"

Indeed, Discepolo's "Que vachache" may simply have been ahead of his time—by three years, to be exact. The great Wall Street crash of 1929 had a less immediate effect on Argentina than it did on Europe and the United States, but its results would be far longer-lasting. The worldwide markets for Argentine exports dried up again, and within a year the country had lost its collective mind—Argentina absolutely could not tolerate anything less than vulgar abundance. The masses revolted against President Hipolito Yrigoyen; old, ineffectual, and "sick to the point of lethargy," according to a *Time* magazine profile, he was like a 1920s clone of Fernando de la Rúa. Like De la Rúa, he had gone to great lengths to project a sober austerity, living in a second-floor apartment above a cigar store instead of in the Casa Rosada. Within half an hour of taking the streets, though, a mob had overrun both his apartment and the Pink House. Portraits of Yrigoyen were hurled into the streets. Two busts of him were dragged out, one decapitated, the other paraded through the streets with a sign: "He's finished!"

The belle époque was gone forever. During the remainder of the twentieth century, the economy would scarcely grow at all and there would be eight military coups. In some respects, the Great Depression was a blow from which Argentina has not yet recovered. The 1930s would be known in Argentina as *la decada infame*, the infamous decade. The pro-British, conservative, landholding elite were now in power, supported by a military regime that purged the unions and sent anyone unfriendly away to the frigid prisons of Patagonia. This paranoid new regime saw Discepolo's unbridled pessimism as an assault on its hegemony, and three of his tangos—"Chorra" ("Criminal"), "Esta noche me emborracho" ("Tonight I'm Getting Drunk"), and the suddenly very relevant "Que vachache"—were summarily banned by the Ministry of the Navy, thus beginning a long and storied relationship between dictatorships and the tango. All three of the banned songs made reference to moral and material misery, and to inequality and social justice. Discepolo acidly replied: "I didn't take the State into account when I wrote my songs." Maybe not, but it certainly wasn't a bad move: the bans, of course, made all three songs wildly popular.

One other shrewd move was necessary to fully launch Discepolo's popularity into the stratosphere: he began working with Carlos Gardel. The pairing might seem odd at first but, in truth, the two men were perfectly matched. Gardel was light to Discepolo's darkness, the yin to his yang. "Que vachache" probably would have been too caustic for mass consumption had it not been for Gardel's sugar-sweet delivery; he might have been the only man on earth who could call Jesus a thief with a smile on his face. Conversely, Gardel might never have appealed to the Argentine taste for the bittersweet, and thus never secured enduring greatness, without Discepolo's pungent tales of woe. Their unlikely but fruitful partnership would produce some of the most memorable tango recordings ever made.

That doesn't mean, however, that the two men liked or even understood each other. This was evidenced by a few short movies Gardel made in which he would sing a tango and then discuss its content with the lyricist. In one such film, Gardel performed one of Discepolo's most acidic songs, "Yira, Yira" ("Hit the streets, hit the streets"):

> *You'll see: all's untrue*
> *No love is real*
> *And the world couldn't care less about you*
> *Hit the streets, hit the streets.*

The ensuing dialogue between Gardel and Discepolo, captured in Simon Collier's biography of the former, speaks volumes about the men's relationship. Gardel comes off as heartbreakingly chirpy, and incredulous at Discepolo's demeanor:

GARDEL: Tell me, Enrique, what did you want to do in this tango, *Yira, yira?*

DISCEPOLO: A song of solitude and despair.

GARDEL: Man! That's just how I understood it.

DISCEPOLO: That's why you sing it so admirably.

GARDEL: But the character portrayed is a good man, isn't he?

DISCEPOLO: Yes, he's a man who has lived with a beautiful hope of fraternity for forty years. And suddenly, one day, when he's forty, he wakes up to the fact that men are beasts!

GARDEL: But he says such bitter things!

DISCEPOLO: You can't imagine that he's going to say amusing things—not if he's someone who has waited forty years before waking up.

It does seem that Gardel was bewildered by the tone of the music he was almost single-handedly making famous. Soon after he began working with Discepolo, Gardel professed to a foreign reporter that he found this rapidly flowering Argentine pessimism a bit of a drag. "Buenos Aires is very nice, *Che*, and its Calle Corrientes has an indefinable enchantment that binds us with links of steel. . . . It isn't that I dislike it—far from it! But it tires you out. . . . Our city is terribly monotonous. And the problem is the Argentines themselves, wrapped up in their funereal seriousness. Here people are ashamed to laugh and beg your pardon for doing so. . . . In Europe, by contrast, people are more open. They enjoy themselves better over here."

Perhaps for this reason, Gardel soon began spending most of his time in Europe. In 1932, he left Argentina for what would be the last time. He eventually made his home in France and then the United States, where he briefly pursued a film career. He toured the world but never again saw his Buenos Aires *querido* before his plane crashed in Colombia in 1935.

The news of Gardel's death was greeted with an outpouring of grief and melodrama by almost all porteños. But for Discepolo, it seemed like a kind of liberation. Now, free from that chirping Pollyanna, he was now able to pursue his true instincts. And as the *decada infame* wore on with no sign of a return to the good old days, Argentina craved more and more of the bitter swill that Discepolo knew best how to produce. Discepolo's songs began to address all of these frustrations over the economy, over the elite, with ever greater intensity. Just months after Gardel's death, "Cambalache" was performed for the first time.

Two CARTONEROS WERE LINGERING OUTSIDE IN A DRIVING rain, struggling mightily to fold a giant slab of cardboard, as I burst through the glass-and-wood doors of the Confiteria Ideal and sprinted, two-by-two, up the stairs.

Inside, it was all light, warmth, and noise. Before me was the tango and all its marvels. I looked around and saw no sign of her, so I walked over to the bar. I ordered a whiskey—Johnnie Walker, black-label, no ice—and downed it in one shot. My throat went numb; it felt marvelous. I scanned the room—but cautiously, taking great care not to look any of the women directly in the eye; I didn't want to accidentally *cabaceo* anyone and ruin my chances with Mariela.

Like a mirage, there she was, wearing a tight black dress and fishnet stockings, her lips painted in brilliant red. It was as if she had chosen an ensemble straight out of the tango cliché handbook; this didn't seem like her at all, but I was in no mood to complain. She gave me a peck on the cheek and smiled.

"*Buenas,*" she said softly. "How are you?"

"Fine, fine."

"Did you come alone?" she asked.

I nodded, my heart racing. There was no sign of Daniel.

"You didn't bring Svetlana?" she asked.

"No. . . . "

Mariela shrugged and grinned. "I told her to call you," she said. "I guess she lost her nerve. Crazy Russian. It doesn't matter. *No pasa nada.*"

Behind her, just out of focus, were a hundred people dancing, holding each other.

"Would you like to dance?" I asked.

"No."

"No?"

"That's not how you ask a woman to tango," she scolded me, a teasing grin on her face. "Haven't I taught you any better than that?"

I laughed and turned away. Slowly, my head rotated back around. I flashed my eyebrows in theatrical seduction. This made her giggle. Then I stared into her eyes for a long moment—utterly serious now—and gave her a slow nod.

"Very good," she whispered. "Now we can dance."

She offered her hand, and off we went.

Had this been Hollywood, at that moment I would have danced the tango of my life. There would have been all kinds of wild *ganchos* and *barridas* and flourishes, and the song would have ended with her perfectly positioned in my arms, her right leg wrapped around my chest, both of us breathing heavily and staring into each other's eyes as the audience applauded in awe. But that was not the tango that I loved—and the truth is that I don't remember anything extraordinary about that particular dance itself. I mostly walked, doing nothing more complex than what El Tigre had taught me on my first day. I moved *confidently*, with purpose, and that was good enough. I listened to the song's rhythm, moved in, and for a shining moment I forgot about all the squalor and rancor just outside the milonga's doors. For those three minutes, it was as if nobody else existed, as if the crisis had never happened. As the song ended, I peeked at Mariela's face and saw that her eyes were pressed tightly shut.

She pulled away and smiled—sincerely, and with enormous pride.

"You've become a marvelous dancer," she said. "Who would have believed it?"

Perfect. I closed my eyes and leaned in to kiss her.

There was no one there.

"Would you like to go meet everybody else?"

My eyes opened back up. Suddenly, Mariela was three steps away.

"Come on!" she said, smiling warmly, apparently ignorant of what had just—what had *not* just happened. She motioned for me to follow her.

We weaved through the crowded dance floor. I kept grasping for her hand but she was several paces ahead of me and I couldn't catch up. Finally, we reached a large table on the unfashionable back wall, in the corner by the bathroom.

"Everyone," she declared with a grand sweep of the hand, "I want you to meet Brian."

Sitting at the table were about a dozen men, all in their twenties or early thirties, all of them of different nationalities. It looked like a particularly disgruntled meeting of the Security Council of the United Nations. There were three Asian men. Two African-looking blacks were sipping frozen piña coladas. A group of American guys in blue jeans and Keds were slumped over at the very end of the table. Everyone glared at me with pungent jealousy.

"Okay, Theo," Mariela said, pointing to a vaguely Greek-looking man sitting in the corner. "Let's go practice that *molinete* we learned in class last Thursday."

Elated, Theo leapt to his feet. Mariela took him by the hand and, without so much as a word to me, led him out to the dance floor where they began to soldier bravely through the *paso básico*.

My head turned back toward the table as it finally dawned on me who these men were.

I meekly took my seat next to a Korean man of about thirty-five. He had a Mickey Mouse backpack hanging from his shoulder, and he surveyed the scene while squinting through thick, horn-rimmed glasses.

We sat there in silence. When we weren't glaring at each other, we were fixated on Mariela.

"She beautiful," the Korean sighed.

"Yes," I allowed. "She very beautiful."

SHE'S A WHORE ANYWAY," EL DANDY MUTTERED.

"That's not true," El Nene protested, suddenly very upset. "Mariela is a very intelligent girl, very kind."

"What did you say?" I asked, staring at El Nene. "How do you know her?"

For a moment, I thought I saw sweat forming on his forehead. "From your descriptions, of course," he replied. "Why?"

I slammed back another glass of bourbon. Everyone at the table was looking at me with great concern.

"Go find yourself another one," El Dandy offered. "There are thousands of women in Argentina."

I rolled my eyes. "Dandy," I said. "Can I ask you a personal question?"

"Naturally." His knee bounced about nervously.

"Have you ever been in love?"

"Of course!" he replied. "I fall in love every time I go to the milonga!"

He said this grandly, but his shoulders immediately slumped, and in short order El Dandy was staring forlornly across the room. I had been cruel, and I knew it.

"You're the ones who taught me to drink like this," I said accusingly.

Everyone stared at me, severely.

"Why are you guys friends with me anyway?" I slurred.

El Nene smiled. "We've been trying to corrupt you," he said in English. "And from the looks of it, we've done a fine job."

I staggered up from my chair. What had I become? I surveyed the room. Maybe I was delusional from all the booze, but at that moment it seemed as if every woman at the milonga was staring at me, hungrily. I blinked several times, but the illusion held. Somehow, I felt simultaneously drunk, jealous, arrogant, and thoroughly heartbroken—apparently, I had finally attained the perfect state of mind for success at the tango. Preposterously, I had my pick of any woman in the room. I had no problem affecting a *cabaceo* toward the opposite side of the room.

She immediately rose to her feet, smiled, and made her way over to me.

And then, as we began to dance, I heard what sounded like a distant, dull, metallic pinging.

"Like gunshots," someone muttered.

"Oh, go fuck yourself," another man snorted, grinning maniacally over his shoulder. "You've never fired a gun before in your life, you coward!"

Their raucous laughter was swept away by the circular current of the crowd. I tried to concentrate on my steps and keep time with the staccato rhythm of the piano. But there it lingered, still, the grating, repetitive sound of metal on metal. And it seemed to be getting closer.

My eyes wandered toward the balcony. Outside, the leaves glittered in the soft copper glow of the streetlights. A brisk summer wind, gusting in straight from Patagonia, made the tablecloths in the room flutter like white flags. Then, I abruptly lost my focus and my partner very nearly went crashing to the floor. "Ay!" she yelped, wobbling on three-inch heels. As she did her best to glare a hole in the side of my skull, I led her through a final, half-hearted series of *ochos*, now praying for the song to please just end.

Mercifully, with a crescendo of screaming violins, an abrupt crash of the piano, and then silence, my wish was granted, giving way only to the sound of the relentless *clang clang clang clang*.

I pulled away from my partner and gave her my best apologetic, drunken grin. "Did I break anything?" I asked.

She was brunette, leggy, maybe thirty-five, and not unattractive in a low-cut, flower-print dress. But her eyes seemed weary, and she looked at me as if I was a movie she had seen a thousand times before. "Go ahead," she sighed with a gentle smile, gesturing toward the balcony. "Go ahead and see if your revolution has started yet."

She pivoted, still a bit wobbly on her heels, and clop-clopped away.

As I walked out onto the club's balcony, the incessant pounding grew louder. By now, most members of the Council were leaning over the railing, pensively sipping their whiskeys, and whispering to each other. I pushed through the crowd, peered over the edge, and. . . .

"There!" El Gil hissed, pointing down the street.

Sure enough, on a fourth-floor balcony a block away there stood the cause of the calamity: a fat old lady in a red wig and a hot-pink muumuu. She held a cooking pot in one hand, a large metal spoon in the other, and she was zealously banging the two together, like her life depended on it. She also appeared to be screaming something. Or was it some kind of chant? I stood and enjoyed the spectacle, amused— and a bit relieved that this wasn't *it* after all. After a long while, the woman apparently grew tired, put down the pot, and shuffled back into her apartment.

And yet, to the surprise of everyone, the noise continued unabated.

"It's the whole city," someone was saying. "*Cacerolazo.*"

"It's ending, it's ending."

I felt a giant hand on my shoulder, and the hair on the back of my neck stood up.

It was El Tigre. "Do you want a whiskey?" he asked me.

I shook my head no.

"Bad choice," El Tigre grumbled, turning his face back toward the warm glow of the dance hall, "but we've got to deal with this *somehow*. Let's all go dance a tango."

DISCEPOLO WROTE HIS MASTERPIECE IN 1935 FOR THE MOVIE *El alma del bandoneon*, starring Libertad Lamarque, the Argentine Rita Hayworth. As a snapshot of that moment in Argentine history, it was extraordinarily perceptive. Similarly, as a synthesis of the Argentine character, then and now, "Cambalache" is sheer genius.

From the classic immigrant's lament that his previous status in the home country no longer mattered. . . .

Nobody cares if you were born honest

. . . to the belief that only begging for handouts from the government could yield a fortune. . . .

If you don't cry, you don't get to nurse

. . . and the certainty that only those who steal can get ahead. . . .

Today it's the same to be law-abiding as it is to be a traitor. . . .
If one lives with honor, or robs in his ambition

. . . what the old Marxist salesman outside Retiro told me on my second day in Buenos Aires was absolutely true: there is no other song more worthy of being called Argentina's "national anthem."

With this tour de force, Discepolo had reached the point where he transcended the tango. The song penetrated so deeply in the popular imagination that, in the decades to come, "Cambalache" would have the singular honor of being banned by each and every Argentine military regime. Discepolo was now a thoroughly political figure, and, like celebrities have always done, he used his fame as an activist in leftist politics, a bit like an Argentine Sean Penn. True to the philosophy of "Cambalache," and that of many of his compatriots, Discepolo usually shunned constructive political discourse, believing that no one was capable of fighting for the virtuous underdog. For many years, Discepolo spent most of his energy opposing things: he was antimilitary, antidemocratic, anticapitalist, anticommunist, pretty much anti-everything . . . until, finally, like a miracle, he finally found his muse.

Juan Domingo Perón could have been a character in one of Discepolo's tangos. His great-grandfather was a Sardinian immigrant who had made a good name for himself as a merchant; however, by the time Juan was born, the family had fallen on hard times. Juan's father eked out a meager living as the overseer of a sheep ranch on the bleak steppes of Patagonia. His mother, who was half-Indian, was barely past puberty and not yet married when she had her two sons. Juan's formative years were spent among other Discepolian characters: criminals, runaways, drunks, and occasionally the odd gaucho. Only the unique upward mobility of the military was able to lift him out of this base existence and on to a respectable career. Perón excelled in the military, where he became a skilled boxer and fencer; he was later sent as an attaché to Germany and Italy. Years after the war ended, Perón was still referring to Mussolini as "the greatest man of our century." Whatever he thought about Hitler, he mostly kept to himself.

Perón understood the true soul of his country better than any politician before or since. "To govern Argentina, you have to put on a Gardel smile," he once declared. Perón even took the unprecedented step of admitting publicly that he liked the tango (though that did not stop him from banning lyrics from artists whom he didn't care for). Indeed, Perón ruled as if he had listened to every single angry tango written over the previous three decades—every working-class lament, every immigrant's dream—and molded his agenda in response. He took the country's enormous wealth and gave it—literally gave it—to the disaffected workers and immigrants, the sons of *compadritos* and gauchos, the underclass who had been aggrieved since the country's inception, but particularly since the Depression took hold. He nationalized the railways, taking them away from the hated British. (Perón acquired them for 2.5 billion pesos worth of reserves; being Argentina, this was paid for with a mix of gold nuggets and beef.) He evicted the "elite" Supreme Court and penned a new "social justice" Constitution. He bestowed paid vacations and a fully fledged welfare state upon the lower classes. All the while, he shook his ass in the face of the elite. When Perón presented his ambitious plan to do all these things, he chose to do so at ground zero for rich Argentina—the Teatro Colón—and he filled the glamorous opera house with trade union officials in shirt sleeves.

Most Argentines today don't make a direct association between Perón and the tango—testimony, perhaps, to the effectiveness of the draconian censorship that would follow Perón's presidency—but the relationship between the two was in fact quite remarkable. Perón was happy to be photographed in the company of musicians and occasionally attended tango festivals. He quoted liberally and often from *Martin Fierro*, the epic poem of gaucho lore. *Lunfardo* slang was sprinkled into his speeches. Several historians have pointed out that Perón frequently touched on familiar tango themes in his speeches; the Argentine poet Luis Franco marveled at Perón's "spiritual affinity with tango lyrics." Indeed, he spoke of nostalgia for mama and the scarcity of women almost as often as he did of social justice and privilege. As

Perón rose to power, when he addressed the crowd at the Plaza de Mayo on October 17, 1945, he said: "I would embrace you as I would my mother, because you have had the same travails and the same thoughts that my poor old lady must have felt in those days." His style might have been more "Mi noche triste" than "Cambalache," but the message was unmistakable.

Perón had a tango singer's flair for the melodramatic that helps keep him relevant today. Late at night, when there are no more protests or traffic accidents to cover live, Crónica will still often show old black-and-white film clips from his most famous speeches. Perón thunders from the balcony of the Casa Rosada while a crowd of hundreds of thousands ebbs and flows down below. Grown men climb on lampposts in the Plaza de Mayo, hold banners, and chant while Perón flings his arms about. Curiously, the clips usually have no sound—it seems that Crónica shows them not out of enduring sympathy for Perón's politics but because, more than a half-century later, the man still makes for damn good TV.

For tips on showmanship, Perón could rely on the advice of a professional actress: his wife, Eva. As any fan of Andrew Lloyd Webber or Madonna knows, "Evita" Duarte de Perón was a poor, illegitimate country girl who slept her way to the top. It was said (but never proven) that a performance by the tango singer Agustin Magaldi in Junin led a fifteen-year-old Evita to move to Buenos Aires. Upon arrival in the big city, she parlayed a modest career as a B-movie and radio actress into a relationship with Juan Perón. Her popularity quickly eclipsed that of her husband, and she fought ardently for the *descamisados*—"the shirtless ones"—who formed their political base. More than a virtuous passion for the poor, however, it seemed to be a hatred for the rich that really drove Evita. In her memoir she wrote: "I remember I was very sad for many days when I discovered that in the world there were poor people and rich people; and the strange thing is that the existence of the poor didn't cause me as much pain as the knowledge that at the same time there were people who were rich." This was as close to a statement of philosophy as you could find. She gave hundreds of millions of dollars away through her foundation and inflamed the class hatred that had been simmering in Argentina ever since the gauchos began trickling into outer Buenos Aires. "Shall we burn down the Barrio Norte?" she would scream to the crowds. "Shall I give you fire?"

Evita was effective, no doubt. But as one of his main propagandists against the rich and powerful, Perón had help from Mr. Cambalache himself. Discepolo was a frequent presence in the Casa Rosada, often advising Perón on crucial matters. This was enormously controversial, because many of his fellow artists and intellectuals were being persecuted at the time. Oswaldo Pugliese, a tango composer and Communist, was imprisoned. Libertad Lamarque, the same actress who had helped launch "Cambalache" to fame, felt obliged to seek exile in Mexico because of her running feud with Evita. Yet Discepolo still clung to Perón like a security blanket, defending himself using his trademark bile and epic language.

"Well look," he told an interviewer, "let me say it once and for all. I didn't invent Perón. I'll tell you this once so that I can be done with this impulse of goodwill that I am following in my desire to free you a little of so much bullshit. The truth: I didn't invent Perón or Evita, the miraculous one. They were born as a reaction to your bad governments. I didn't invent Perón, or Evita, or their doctrines. They were summoned as defense by a people who you and yours submerged in a long path of misery. They were born of you, by you and for you."

Still, Discepolo was unapologetic: "For years and years the inhabitants of the suburbs lived in that absurd comfort: The humiliating comfort of the *conventillo*! A rusty symphony . . . a world where the trash can was a trophy and the rat was a domestic animal! I remember things. I weigh things now, and the balance goes over right away to the ancient misery that has now been overcome. Because the new Argentine conscience had an idea. You know what idea? That the humble also had the right to live in a clean and peaceful house—not in the promiscuity of the *conventillo*."

In the dark years that have passed since, Argentines have assigned all sorts of magical qualities to Juan and Evita Perón; even their sworn enemies (and there are still millions of them) grudgingly admit that the Peróns were geniuses when it came to politics and understanding the Argentine soul. But it seems that, above all, Perón had the good fortune of being the last Argentine leader to preside over a period of sheer abundance. At that time, Argentina was a creditor nation, owed $2 billion by Britain alone. Simply put, Perón was everything to everybody because he could afford to be. In fact, there was so much abundance that he could not give away the money fast enough. Every Argentine government for the next half-century would try—and fail—to live up to Peron's example. "We have the Central Bank full of gold and we don't know where to put it any more," Perón told a group of foreign visitors. "The passages are full of piles of gold."

Until, that is, the money started to run out—again. Before Perón's ascent to power, *Time* magazine had observed: "Argentina automatically renews its fabulous grain and cattle wealth with every cycle of the seasons, and no amount of mismanagement on high can seem to ruin it." Perhaps a few decades before, this would have been true—but the Peróns' zeal for class warfare succeeded in destroying any and all investments. By Perón's second term, the country was beset by beef shortages. Just like that, the money was gone.

M OMENTS BEFORE THE WHOLE CITY BEGAN BANGING THEIR pots and pans, President De la Rúa had appeared on television in one last, vain effort to calm the country. Whether it was denial, incompetence, drunkenness, or a base desire to finally push Argentina over the threshold into free fall that motivated him, De la Rúa's words merely added fuel to the fire. Reading a speech that had been penned by his son, who was most famous for dating the Colombian rock star Shakira, De la Rúa blamed that day's supermarket riots on "enemies of the republic who want to take advantage of things by trying to sow discord and violence, seeking to create a chaos that gives them room to achieve what they couldn't via elections." He then declared a state of siege, a move that disastrously recalled the military dictatorships of years past. That was the moment when Argentines decided they'd had enough.

From the balcony, scotches in hand, we watched as the streets filled with people like a slowly rising tide. People of all ages serenely walked out the front doors of their apartment buildings; old ladies, men with canes, teenagers dressed in all black, young fathers with children perched on their shoulders. Some brought their dogs with them on a leash. The people milled about, chatting easily but grimly with their neighbors, seemingly waiting for instructions on where to go next. It looked as if they were all going on a midnight picnic. It was all so spontaneous, so civilized, that it took me a few minutes to realize that I was in fact witnessing the formation of a lynch mob.

We stood there, dumbfounded. All the silver tongues had gone silent. El Nene's fingers tapped lightly on the iron railing of the balcony. Eyes were flickering furtively about, everybody watching everybody, just like inside the milonga—except now, outside, something entirely different and more important was at stake. This was one of those moments where people took sides: you either stepped forward or you didn't, and you forever remembered your choice.

El Tigre had momentarily come back outside, but he was the first to blink. He snorted loudly and crinkled his nose in a very public exhibition of disgust. "I don't do politics," he muttered. And with not a word more, he disappeared inside.

Everyone turned around and stared, watching as El Tigre waddled—he had gained a prodigious amount of weight in recent months—back into the salon. He collapsed into his chair, looking completely disconsolate, and resumed drinking.

"*Obvio*," El Nene muttered, turning back to face the street, completely nonplussed. "El Tigre, with all his dollars. What does he care? He never had a stake in this country anyway."

Meanwhile, the crowd on the street seemed to have abruptly decided on a destination and began shuffling toward Avenida Garay, headed downtown.

"I'm going downstairs," El Chino #1 declared gruffly. "I've been waiting for this moment for fifty years."

With that, the floodgates opened and everyone else on the balcony began filing toward the door.

El Nene turned to me and smiled, apology in his eyes. "This isn't your country," he said. "You don't have to go."

"Of course he does!" El Dandy interrupted before I could respond. "If he's one of us now!" I smiled gratefully, and then, as if trying to eliminate any doubt I might have had, El Dandy reached into the breast pocket of his vanilla-colored suit and pulled out his pen, the same one he'd always mindlessly twirled around while sitting at our table. He grinned and took off the cap to reveal a long, sharp blade.

"*La concha de la lora!*" El Gil exclaimed. "It's a knife!"

"Have you always carried that?" I asked.

El Dandy shrugged. "Waiting for a night like tonight, I suppose."

He gingerly handed the knife over to El Chino #2, who cradled it in his hands like it was dynamite.

I saw a glint in El Dandy's eyes. Now El Nene had the look, too. It was bloodlust—the inexperienced kind. It occurred to me that none of these men had ever experienced real violence in their lives.

"Well, I can't miss this!" El Gil declared cheerily.

El Nene simply nodded.

"Let's go," El Dandy declared, suddenly the alpha-dog.

We left the balcony and walked past the main salon. On my way out, I caught a glimpse of El Tigre. He had already found a dance partner and was whirling about with complete abandon like he had forgotten the whole thing.

Upon reaching the street, we turned down Avenida Garay and then onto Paseo Colón and headed directly for the plaza. It was hot as a furnace, with no breeze, which seemed to be riling up the crowd even further. The leaves on the trees were wilting, sickly. None of us said a word. We just looked at the crowd. People stared ahead, walking along in grim silence. Everyone was sweating profusely. For the first time since I had been there, the Argentines seemed to have a sense of purpose. We passed the old engineering school, the ill-fated monument to Evita Perón, its columns blazing white in the night. We passed the dueling red and beige mansions that once belonged to two obscenely rich brothers and were now the Agriculture Ministry. We passed Puerto Madero, the old port that had been built for no reason at all and had been partially restored by Carlos Menem during the 1990s. And, finally, we turned to the left, passed the Economy Ministry (still pocked with bullet holes from a revolt against Perón), walked up the hill, and entered the plaza.

It was an astonishing sight. Thousands of people were there, beating pots and pans hoisted high in the air. Many were jumping up and down like they were at a soccer game. Everybody was clapping. Some had made banners, a few of them with hammers and sickles. But otherwise, remarkably, this appeared to be a middle-class revolution. News cameras and bright lights were lined up on the side of the plaza. I wondered what the headline on Crónica was right now.

"Thief! Return what you robbed!" one blonde woman was yelling.

We stood off to the side, watching.

"Cavallo is dead!" someone yelled. "Cavallo is dead!"

Everyone looked around. Was it true?

"That's a pity," El Nene rumbled. "I'd have done it with my bare hands."

El Dandy had a metal flask that he passed around.

It was nearing 4 A.M. now.

"What caused this?" I asked.

"De la Rúa said he was going to become a dictator, and the people revolted!" an old man turned around and answered.

The crowd began chanting: "*Hijo de puta! Hijo de puta!*— Motherfucker! Motherfucker!" The civilized tone was now gone; it seemed that all the women and children had left the plaza and been replaced by young, shirtless men. Some of them wore bandannas over their faces. A few had slingshots. Everyone was leaning forward, like they were about to charge the Casa Rosada. Impossibly, more people came pouring in, even though it didn't appear there was any room for them. The crowd lurched forward.

"*Que pesado*," El Dandy said. "How dull. *Muchachos, nos vamos?*"

I stared at him in disbelief. "Leave, now?"

"Why not?"

"You've lost your mind," I said, suddenly feeling very disappointed. "Why now?"

"We've seen this movie before," El Nene said, nodding his head. "Let's go to a *boliche* and find some girls."

"Nothing's going to happen anyway," El Dandy said. "They can throw De la Rúa into the Río de la Plata and it wouldn't change anything."

"This is total bullshit," El Chino #1 agreed, his arms folded, looking at the sea of people. "Girls would help the situation immensely."

I stared at El Nene, dumfounded. He looked away, noncommital.

"How can you think about women right now?" I asked.

"What else would we be thinking about?"

"Argentina!"

"Nooooo!" They all laughed in unison.

"*Que boludo*," El Dandy sighed.

The crowd was starting to sway. The chanting had reached a fevered pitch.

"You won't miss the action anyway. Nothing will happen until tomorrow."

"Which milonga are we going to?" I asked. "The Ideal?"

"No milonga tonight!" El Dandy declared, still mysteriously happy. "A special night calls for a special place. Where shall we go, boys?"

El Nene sighed. "Well," he said hesitantly, "I know just the place."

THINGS WERE ALREADY FALLING APART BY THE TIME PERÓN sought reelection in 1951, and Discepolo was determined not to go down without a fight. The relationship between Discepolo and Perón originated the radio program *I Think*

. . . *and I Say What I Think* on which the minstrel of the Buenos Aires streets had a dialogue with "Mordisquito," an imaginary opponent to the government. Discepolo wrote and performed the dialogue himself. He even submitted drafts of each night's performance directly to Perón for final approval. It turned out to be an extraordinary radio hit. Here, to everyone's surprise, one of the most caustic artists of all time turned his talents to propaganda. It was truly jaw-dropping in its pessimism, like "Cambalache" but without the subtlety:

"So, before you didn't care about anything, and now you care about everything. You went from castaway to financier without even getting off the boat. You, yes, you . . . and yet you protest."

"Ah! There is no tea!"

"That is tremendous. Look, what a problem! There is milk, there is plenty of milk. Your kids, who once had to take turns just to look at cream, now can go off to school and take the whole cow with them."

"But there's no tea!"

"And according to you, you can't live without tea. . . . The conquest of human dignity means nothing to you! I respect you, but me, me you're not even going to look at. See you tomorrow! Yes?"

Argentines were shocked. Soon, the entire country was tuning in to the radio. The extraordinary thing was that Discepolo was essentially mocking Perón's opponents for practicing the exact sort of pessimism that had become his trademark. His tangos were turned on their head, in the ramblings of a man who, in retrospect, was evidently sick:

"Why do you speak if you don't know anything? We're living the Technicolor of the glorious days and you want me to switch them for the negative rolls of pessimism, gossip, suspicion and depression. No! I know you! Ooh, I know you! You are, look, you are the one who has no facts on your side, so you use rumors. . . . "

And so on. Discepolo did thirty-seven such programs. Unbelievably, they worked to great effect. Perón was reelected on November 11, 1951. Years later, Perón would credit the victory to two main factors: the women's vote, and to "Mordisquito."

Even before that election, the hate mail had started coming. People sent messages like "E. S. D. rest in peace." Others mailed feces. Discepolo's peers, many of whom had been blacklisted and forced into exile, could not forgive him; for them, and much of Argentina, he was Jane Fonda at Hanoi times a thousand. Discepolo stopped answering the telephone. The final straw, according to Sergio Pujol's fantastic biography *Discepolo* came when the miserable wretch ran into a former friend, the actor Orestes Caviglia, on his way to a restaurant in Buenos Aires. Caviglia had been blacklisted by Perón and sought exile in Uruguay; he sneaked back into Argentina by boat, wearing a fake beard, a hat, and glasses, to visit a granddaughter who was sick with polio. Upon returning for a quick visit to Buenos Aires, he heard Discepolo's program on the radio.

Discepolo spotted Caviglia on the street, called after him and opened his arms to give him a hug. Caviglia ducked his embrace, spit with all his might on the sidewalk, and declared: "You are a *porqueria*." It was the same *lunfardo* word, meaning "piece of shit," that Discepolo had so famously used to describe the entire world in the first verse of "Cambalche."

Discepolo stood there, frozen, heartbroken. It was a moment straight from one of his tangos; the long-suffering, bitter, self-righteous underdog who turned his back on the wealthy, well-connected, unscrupulous sell-out. In an instant, Discepolo must have realized he had become everything he hated, everything his work had stood against.

"That was when Discepolo fell apart," Pujol wrote. From that moment on, "it was his ghost that kept walking." A week after the elections, Discepolo came down with a severe flu. Never a hearty eater, he gave up food altogether; some days his only meal was a bottle of whisky. Before long, he weighed only 80 pounds. He stopped listening to tangos in the morning and would only lie in bed, nearly catatonic. The best doctors in Buenos Aires could not decipher what was wrong with him. His lifelong companion, Ana Luciana Devis, would later write that he "slowly died of bitterness."

On his deathbed, Discepolo would go on riffs of irony and hatred that Devis later described as "laughably pathetic." On December 23, 1951, less than two months removed from Perón's fleeting victory, Discepolo died in his Buenos Aires apartment at the age of fifty.

———

THE MULTITUDE AT THE CASA ROSADA IS STARTING TO LOSE control," the Radio 10 reporter was saying. "There is still no response from President Fernando. . . . "

"*Apagá esa mierda!*" El Dandy bellowed, furious, banging his fist on the back of the taxi driver's seat.

"Excuse me, sir," the cabbie said, his voice cracking, "but this is a historic moment for the country and I think we have an obligation to. . . . "

"Turn that shit off!" El Dandy repeated. I had never seen him so angry, not even during the debate over the merits of the gaucho. "Turn it off!"

The taxi driver angrily obliged just as we pulled up in front of a belle époque building in Recoleta. It was a structure I'd never noticed before, just two blocks away from the cemetery and down the street from an Al Queso, Queso. The fare was six pesos. El Dandy asked the cabbie if he had change for a 100-peso bill, knowing full well that he wouldn't. "*Sori, viejo,*" El Dandy replied with a shrug of the shoulders. "That's all I've got. I guess we'll have to pay you next time." The taxi sped away with a screech that must have woken the whole neighborhood—the rest of the city might have been downtown demonstrating at the plaza, but Recoleta had stayed home. El Dandy turned to El Nene, shrugged, and laughed.

"Puerto Colón," read the sign above two wooden doors with circular, opaque windows, like the entrance to an outrageously tacky yacht.

A red digital clock hanging from the awning down the street blinked 05:15. My eyes felt like they were on fire. I couldn't remember ever having been more tired.

The four of us staggered inside like we were entering a saloon in an old John Wayne movie. But Puerto Colón was a time warp not to the 1940s but the 1970s—the place was decorated like the inside of a cruise ship that had not been refurbished since the era of shag carpeting and lava lamps. In the corner, a man with the biggest mullet I'd ever seen was playing Phil Collins songs on a stand-up keyboard and singing with great passion into a crackly microphone. Notably, he appeared to be the only male working there; the rest of the staff, from the bartenders on down, was female, scantily dressed, and slathered in thick makeup. There seemed to be an awful lot of waitresses.

A few Japanese businessmen in suits sat in the shadows in the opposite corner, drunkenly singing along with the keyboardist. "Su-su-sudioooo!!!" the Japanese businessmen yelled, laughing riotously.

A waitress in her fifties brought us some cocktail napkins and a crusty menu.

"This place is more meager each time I see it," El Nene muttered darkly.

"Don't be so *pesado*," El Dandy retorted. "Puerto Colón is legendary. Do you remember the nights we used to have here after Salon Canning? When that girl Deborah and her. . . . "

"Yes, yes, I remember," El Nene interrupted him, shaking his head. "I've tried to forget, but I have to remember."

We were soon joined on our plaid couch by four women. One of them, younger than the rest but with pitch-black circles under her eyes, put her hand on my leg, stroked my thigh for a moment, and then smiled.

"I'll be your waitress tonight," she began. "What would you like?"

"To drink?" I asked.

She nodded, her smile widening.

I froze.

Finally, El Nene leaned over and answered for me. "He'd like a Johnny Walker, black label," he said, firmly in control, as always.

The "waitress" stood up and winked. "I'll be back with your drink," she cooed, "and then we can really *talk*."

I sat there, rubbing my head, looking at the door, then back at the boys, having my thousandth "what the hell am I doing here?" moment of the night. El Chino #1 was slumped in a chair by himself, sound asleep. El Dandy was excitedly trying to shoot a *cabaceo* at one of the fifteen waitresses standing in the corner by the businessmen. One of the Japanese empresarios had pulled out his wallet and was brandishing a roll of $100 bills. Everyone in the room watched the cash hungrily, myself included.

My eyes met Nene's. He saw the look on my face and he shrugged with exhaustion, looking every bit his sixty-five years. "What else are we doing to do?" he sighed, and then he turned his back on me for the rest of the night.

My waitress came back with my whiskey and sat back down beside me, resting her head on my shoulder. The weight felt warm, reassuring. I couldn't quite tell whether she was attractive or not—maybe it was the light, maybe it was the hour, maybe it was the booze—but she smelled like oranges and she was very tall. I looked down at the top of her head and, to my enormous surprise, found myself considering it. . . .

"This is my first night here," she said, batting her eyes at me, lying with alarming expertise. "I'm very nervous."

"What was your job before?"

"I was a dancer."

Some things are the same the world over, I thought.

"How do you know these men?" she asked.

"Oh, we're friends."

"They seem very old to be your friends," she said, puzzled.

"They teach me things," I said. One sip of the whiskey and I was drunk. "They teach very important things."

"Like what?"

"Like how to tango."

Her eyes brightened. "Tango!" she shrieked, shocked. Everyone in the room turned and stared. "I've never danced a tango in my life. Will you show me?"

She jumped to her feet and ran over to the parquet floor in the corner.

El Dandy had closed the deal with his "waitress" in record time, and the two of them were getting up to leave. He threw his cream-colored sport jacket over his shoulder, grabbed his white cane, and smiled like all the world's problems had just melted away. "Oh, show the girl how to dance!" he admonished me cheerily. "You're a *profesor* now. Our mission is complete!"

El Dandy put his arm over the prostitute's shoulder, laughed heartily, and disappeared out the front door.

I turned around, and the girl was standing there, waiting for me in an empty space at the bar right in front of the keyboardist, who was now performing "Bette Davis Eyes." The original 1980s version had been incomprehensible enough, but this keyboardist was apparently no *anglo-argentino*, and he mangled the lyrics with aplomb:

> *She's atrocious, and she know just*
> *What it take to make a throw rush*

She's got many, many, many sighs
She's got Bette Davis eyes.

To the tune of this and other finely altered 1980s hits, I spent the short remainder of the night showing the girl—she never told me her name—a few rudimentary steps of the tango. I also taught her about the *cabaceo* and walked her through all seven phases of the *paso basico*. She laughed and laughed. At 8 A.M., knowing I had just an hour and a half to go home, shower, and get dressed for possibly the most important day of work of my life, I paid my bill and I kissed her on the lips good-bye. It was, by far, the most fun I ever had dancing the tango.

EL DANDY HAD BEEN ABSOLUTELY RIGHT; NOTHING ELSE OF consequence had happened that night after we left the Plaza. Sure, there had been some looting at a McDonald's downtown. Someone had also pumped a few bullets into the house of Chacho Alvarez, the former vice president who had resigned. At about 1:30 A.M., about sixty people tried to set fire to the ex-cabinet chief's garage, and a mob threw trash at the house of Maria Julia Alsogaray, who had a reputation as Menem's most corrupt minister. It was clear, yet again, that the public was not angry at any one particular politician or party, but the whole lot of them. Apart from that, after a few more hours of yelling, everyone (except us, apparently) had gone home for a few hours of sleep.

Once the city woke up again, however, the crowd re-turned to the Plaza de Mayo, and this time it smelled blood. By noon, on a steaming December summer day, tens of thou-sands of people had gathered. All of the men at the protest were either completely shirtless or wearing full suits; the crowd seemed to be an odd mix of bankers and *piqueteros*. They lurched ever closer to the Casa Rosada, screaming, chanting, jumping, like it was some kind of carnival. Then, at around 1 P.M., the *policia federal* received orders to clear the plaza. Dozens of police on horseback came galloping into the square wielding batons. Among those injured in the ensuing melee were several members of the human rights group Madres de la Plaza de Mayo, made up of mothers of those who had disappeared during the 1976–1983 military dicta-torship. Water cannons sprayed the crowd as people ran, ter-rified, to escape the plaza.

Word spread quickly that the *represion* had begun; the protests were no longer a party, and the kids stayed at home. At commuter stations, people promptly deboarded their trains and sprinted to their offices. At offices in the *microcen-tro*, people were glued to their windows. Most of them were sent home by midday. Elsewhere around the city, police would stand around and, when they saw protesters coming, start frantically ordering shopkeepers to close the metal shutters on their doors. Much of the supermarket looting stayed in the outer ring of Buenos Aires, but some of it trick-led into the downtown *capital federal* area. Most of those killed were men under twenty-five, shot by supermarket owners on their way in. There was a thirty-five-year-old widow with seven kids who died. An eleven-year-old girl also got a shotgun blast to the head.

I was safely ensconced in the Reuters office as all this terror unfolded. I watched most of it on Crónica—TRAGEDY IN THE PLAZA DE MAYO—as I worked on a story with dark predictions about what was in the cards for Argentina. Yet, throughout the day De la Rúa was almost entirely silent; newspapers reported that he spent his lunch watching the revolt on TV (one assumes it was Todo Noticias and not Crónica) while calmly eating a yogurt. By about 3 P.M. even De la Rúa could no longer ignore the situation. Cognizant of what had happened to Celman, to Yrigoyen, to Perón, to so many others, De la Rúa panicked and ordered the cavalry to attack.

As horses again clattered down Avenida Corrientes, De la Rúa's fate was sealed. In several spots around downtown, the police lost control and opened fire on the crowd. In front of the crumbling mansions, beneath the slowly waving leaves of trees that had been planted a century before, all hell broke loose. Banks and cars were set on fire, so was a McDonald's, and bloody corpses were strewn throughout downtown. By the end of the day, over two dozen people had died. Never mind that in almost any other country in the world (the United States included), a revolt of such proportions under similarly desperate circumstances would have killed not two dozen but (at least) two hundred—this was still intolerable. The deaths only enraged the crowd further. By 5 P.M., as the demonstrators literally pounded on the palace door, De la Rúa, fearing for his life, decided to resign. He hand-wrote his resignation and then, dazed, asked his secretary to please collect the soaps in the presidential bathroom. Only then did he rush up to the roof of the palace, boarded a military helicopter, and was promptly whisked away into anonymity, the eighth president in Argentine history to simply walk away.

There was no vice president to take his place, no clear line of succession, no plan to rescue Argentina from impending doom. It was clear that the pain was really just beginning; a currency devaluation and a debt default surely awaited. Someone would have to step forward and administer the bitter medicine, but it was unclear who. Over the next two weeks, four different presidents would try their luck in the Casa Rosada, with no luck. The country was leaderless, adrift, and the worst was yet to come.

That night, once the news of De la Rúa's resignation had spread, the protests had died down. I was exhausted, but it was a Thursday, so on my way home from the office at 1 A.M. I asked the cabbie to take me by the Niño Bien. For the first time in the club's history, it was closed.

IN THE DARK YEARS AFTER PERÓN FELL, THE TANGO NEARLY went extinct. Argentina slipped into a period of crazy, unrestrained revenge and bloodletting; a country that had once been part of the world withdrew into itself. It was as if someone had closed all the windows at the asylum.

Almost overnight, the tango went from being a symbol of Argentina to something that society was either ashamed of or, worse, apathetic about. What tango existed was driven underground. It was like a return to the pre-Paris days. What made this truly shocking was that most Argentines didn't really seem to miss it; it was as if the tango had been forgotten. Some of this was due to the natural passage of time; the tango was also overtaken by rock and roll. The emerging popularity of television played a role as well; for some people, there was no longer any need to make friends.

But, as usual, it was politics that played the biggest role. Tango was never officially banned, but the dictatorship made it known that anything from the Perón years was now anathema, and the tango suffered by association. Rich, "proper" Argentina believed it was back in charge now, and there was no going back. Juan Domingo Perón's name was forbidden from public display. People were even afraid to speak his name in public— some wise *anglo-argentinos* got around this ban by referring to him only as "Johnny Sunday." And just to show how serious the so-called *revolucion libertadora* was about this ban, the new dictator, Pedro Eugenio Aramburu, sent an army expedition up Mount Aconcagua, the hemisphere's highest peak at 22,800 feet, to topple a bust of Perón. A team of government clerks removed thousands of references to the Perón name from the Buenos Aires telephone book—and it wasn't until later that they discovered that the listing for the Committee to Obtain the Nobel Prize for Perón had accidentally slipped through.

None of this worked, of course. The economy had begun its tailspin. The memory of Perón acquired mystical powers. His memory would hold Argentina hostage for the next three decades. Workers with fresh memories of their six-week paid vacations agitated for his return from exile in Spain. Meanwhile, the old landholding elite—with the military as their protector—sought to make sure that the man never returned.

This struggle turned Argentina into a Sicilian-style mob war zone. Crazy, bizarre, incomprehensible things happened. Perón would briefly return to power, with a woman who had been a cabaret dancer in Panama as the apparent replacement for the deceased Evita. He died, and she became president. The coup that followed would result in a military regime that, in a desperate attempt to wipe out Perón's memory, abducted and killed as many as 30,000 people.

Tango was never officially banned, but close enough. Oppression against the great tango artists of the day was widespread. Soon, the orchestras stopped performing altogether. More concretely, mass gatherings were frequently discouraged. And, in fact, it is said that the regime rigorously enforced a curfew on kids under eighteen—but at tango clubs, not at rock 'n' roll. The overall climate of fear and insanity took its toll. This may have been the era when "show" tango first took form—the milongueros who went abroad and started teaching choreographed moves; prior to that, everything had been improvised.

What tango was left survived as a tired, decadent reminder of a tired, decadent country. The music had always been melancholy, of course; but recordings from the era, and particularly from the 1970s, are not energetic in their bitterness; all the musicians sound as if they were merely exhausted. In recordings from Hugo Diaz, a bandleader during that era, the *bandoneon* practically wheezes, as if demanding to be put out of its misery. Other music survived on censored TV programs like *Grandes Valores del Tango*, where a watered-down version of tango was played with the tacit approval of the military. Tangos that had the unfortunate luck to have been written in the era are bland and awful. The laughably bad "Azucar, pimienta y sal" ("Sugar, Pepper, and Salt"), written in 1972, illustrates how sanitary, and pitiful, tango had become. It goes through the motions of rebellion, trying hard to sound like a tango, blandly giving lip service to rebellion and cigarettes (though not to booze), but the song ultimately reads as if it had endured the black-marker strikes of fifty different censors before making it to the radio:

I love her because she's like that
With her heart of a cricket.
She likes the same things as me:
Coffee and cigarettes,
Sitting at a bar
Or walking without cash
Like that, as she is
Rebellious and angelic!
Like that, as she is
Sugar, pepper, and salt!
And though she's always on the moon
I wouldn't change her for anyone
I feel her like the sun on my skin.
I'm happy in my way
And I like that she loves me
Like that, as she is.
I love her, difficult as she is
With her different world
Her upside-down world doesn't matter
Neither does what they say about me.
Because I love her like that
Like that, as she is
Rebellious and angelic.
Like that, as she is
Sugar, pepper and salt!

It is no wonder that almost every Argentine who came of age from the 1960s to the 1980s detests the tango. Frankly, it is a miracle that tango survived the era at all.

The parallels between the fortunes of the tango and Argentine politics throughout history are truly striking. The coinciding arcs bear repeating: the tango was formed during a time of great turmoil, when Argentina was in its embryonic years; it rose to prominence amid a time of prosperity almost unprecedented in the world; and then it nearly disappeared during the country's darkest hour. This pattern would repeat itself during the early 1980s, when tango came back from the dead.

Just a year after the last dictatorship collapsed and democracy returned to Argentina in 1983, a group of old milongueros unveiled the production that many still credit with sparking the tango's renaissance: a Broadway show named *Forever Tango*. After so many decades of neglect, the production was clearly a visionary endeavor. As *Time* magazine put it when it debuted: "Suppose you wanted to stage a Broadway flop and were casting around for surefire bad ideas. What would you think of? Well, how about this: fifteen mostly middle-aged and sometimes portly Argentines dancing the night away in that hoary old favorite, the tango. Add to that four singers declaring their sorrows in Spanish and an orchestra heavy on *bandoneons*, and the marquee might as well say DISASTER."

Yes, but even after so many years, the dance's magic was apparent. The troupe was formed by several old milonguero couples who had no fame, no name—just love of the music. "We've come to prevent it from dying," said Elvira Santa María, a fifty-six-year-old dancer. They succeeded—the show was an instant hit. And just as had happened when the tango went to Paris in the 1910s, the renewed interest abroad quickly spread back to Argentina. The funny thing was that now a generation wanted to tango—but there was no established way to teach them. That was when classes first started appearing en masse. During the Golden Age, it was something that had been passed seamlessly from one age group to another; now there would need to be formalized education for the first time.

Between 2000 and 2004—the worst years of the Argentine crisis, and the time when I lived there—the number of milongas in Buenos Aires *doubled*. Even when the economy imploded, the vibrancy of the country's culture could not be stamped out. Against all odds, people kept coming back to the tango, a century-old dance that had gone out of style in the 1950s. There was no logical way to explain it. It must have been that damn embrace.

⌐

D*ESAYUNO* WAS A SERIOUS MORNING NEWS SHOW—IT HAD just one puppet behind the anchor desk, and he was allowed to do only traffic reports. The man who delivered the news, Victor Hugo Morales, was a Renaissance man with the chin of a Greek god, who had toured the symphony halls of the world and could fluently hold forth on the relative merits of Mozart and Tchaikovsky. Somehow, this made him the perfect radio play-by-play man for Argentine soccer games, and though my soccer interest was never that high, I would regularly listen to games he called on Radio Continental. I had once listened to his account of a championship game between Boca and Independiente on a road trip home from a friend's wedding deep in the Pampa. Morales was musing dispassionately about the complexities of Boca's triangulation scheme when a midfielder suddenly slipped through the defense and: "*Gooooooooooooooooaal! Goooooooooooooooooooooooooaal!!!!!!* Oooohhhhhhh! Ladies and gentlemen! Ladies and gentlemen, there are newborn babies, and there are shining cities on hills, but ladies and gentlemen there is nothing else in the world as beautiful as a GOAL LIKE THAT! *Gooooooooooooal. . . .* "

Morales was more subdued on this morning as I appeared as a guest on his show. It was the fourth of July, and they wanted someone to explain why we did bizarre things like sing the national anthem and barbecue hot dogs instead of steak. His staff had called Reuters and asked if there were any Americans around. Now I was seated at the anchor desk between Morales and a cheery blonde. At the other end of the table, the fuzzy yellow puppet was eyeing me dubiously.

"But when you're singing the national anthem, why do you place your hand over your heart?" Morales was asking.

"I don't know," I replied.

This disappointed him. "Is it patriotism?"

"Well, yes, of course."

"Because that degree of patriotism is shocking for an Argentine. With this crisis, I'm not sure any of us feel any loyalty to our country these days."

Morales was from Uruguay, but he mostly kept this to himself.

"Do you feel more patriotism because this is the first July fourth since the attack on the twin towers?" he asked.

"Yes, I do."

"Do you ever miss your home country?"

I smiled, thought about this for a moment, and replied: "Well, yes. Sometimes."

With that, the cameras went off.

"You look like an American," Victor Hugo said, "but you seem almost Argentine."

I beamed with pride. "Thank you."

"That's not necessarily a compliment."

I laughed.

"What have you enjoyed most about your time here?"

"The tango," I replied.

He cast his eyes downward and frowned, the weight of the world suddenly upon his shoulders. "The tango," he sighed. "The tango represents everything I love and hate about Argentina."

We sat there for a long moment in silence.

Then, Morales laughed, and suddenly he was a cheery morning TV news anchor again. "An American who dances the tango!" he declared. "Who ever heard of that?" He laughed, checked his hair, and then promptly forgot about me, his attention fully devoted to the action on the other side of the room. "Is the puppet ready to go on?"

J UST BEFORE I LEFT ARGENTINA FOR GOOD, I STOPPED BY Mariela's dance studio for one last class. We had been seeing each other only infrequently in recent months, and we spent more time chatting than dancing. Going to see her in San

Telmo was now less a tango lesson than a visit between old friends—except, as always, I had to pay her when it was all over.

Daniel was nowhere to be seen; there was no explanation for his absence, and none was needed. Mariela and I spent most of the last "class" just comparing our appendix scars. Mine had exploded when I was nineteen, leaving a long, thin, horizontal scar across my abdomen. An Argentine doctor had once asked me, horrified: "Where did you get that done, the Bronx?" (I told him "No, Texas," and he seemed to understand.) Hers, however, was an even longer, vertical scar running well beneath her waistline that was even more poorly rendered than my own.

"I was twelve," she explained, "and the doctors had to hold me down."

"What about anesthetic?" I asked, horrified.

She shrugged. "My parents worry every time I go to the doctor," she said. Then, she caught herself and brightened up. "Are you going to go see your friends at the Niño Bien before you leave?"

I nodded.

"Good," she said. "We're lucky, you know."

"How so?"

"Those men," she said, "are dying. These guys like El Dandy who spend twenty-four hours a day living and breathing the music and the dance, obeying the codes of the tango, lyrics that Gardel sang half a century ago, these men will disappear. That *lifestyle* of the milonguero—honor, the gunfight, the *cabaceo*, that sort of thing—it won't be around in ten or fifteen years. I personally think it's a beautiful, authentic way of life, even if those men can be unbearable."

I decided not to ask her how she knew El Dandy. "Will the tango survive?" I asked.

"Oh yes, of course. The tango will always survive. There is one thing that the tango will never lose: the attractiveness of breaking down that barrier between man and woman. When you're on the street, you see a couple embraced. You associate that with something sexual, romantic. In the tango, that happens, and it's the same thing. You see so many people *unida*, together—but is it romantic? No? Or yes? The fact is that everybody can dance the tango. Everybody can experience that. And that's beautiful."

That seemed like an appropriate moment for us to dance a few final tangos. When I pulled away after the final one, when it was time for me to go home and pack, I saw that she was crying.

"What are you doing?" I said, smiling. I desperately wanted to reach out and wipe the tears away, but I knew I couldn't. "I'm not worth crying over," I said softly. "I'm just your student."

"I know, I know," she sobbed. "But it's impossible not to feel this way about someone who you dance with so much. You're not the only one—I cry like this when all my favorite students leave. But this was real."

On my way out the door, I handed Mariela forty pesos. She winked, gave me a big kiss on the cheek, and then turned back inside.

YOU SHOULD HAVE SLEPT WITH HER," EL NENE SIGHED LATER that night.

"No doubt," El Dandy added, shaking his head in shame.

"I know you might not believe it," I said, "but there are some things even you guys don't understand."

EPILOGUE

AFTER I LEFT BUENOS AIRES, I SPENT A YEAR LIVING IN Mexico City, where I was the most grotesque creature imaginable—a Texan with an Argentine accent. I wore too many sweaters, I couldn't hold my tequila, I insisted on saying *ciao* instead of *adios*, and I had a strong urge to kiss everyone I met on the cheek, including men. (This last behavior was grounds for justifiable homicide in Mexico, and everywhere else in Latin America for that matter.) Making the situation worse, I was lily-white and blond—certainly not an issue in Argentina, but in Mexico I discovered that I resembled the *gringo* villain in every Mexican film ever made. Many of the people I met—the *chilangos*, as Mexico City residents are called—were hip, modern, and edgy; if the porteños were Paris chic, the *chilangos* were Los Angeles cool, with absolutely no patience for preening or intellectual airs. Each time I opened my mouth, and the first double-L came out as an Argentine *zh*, the Mexicans looked like they wanted to stab me in the stomach.

Every day at the office I sat next to a wiry Mexican man with a goatee who liked arthouse films and Patron tequila, showed up for work every day with a hangover, and addressed me exclusively and often as "*pinche* fucking *gringo*." Whenever we collaborated on a project, he would begin our conversation with "*Cheeeeeeeeee*," leering at me over his desk, doing his best sneering Argentine/Italian mobster impression. "*Boluuuuudoooooo*," he crooned. Everybody in the office would crack up, and I would sink ever further into my chair.

"¡*Qué extraordinario*!" he mused one day. "A mixture of Texan and Argentine! Could you possibly be more arrogant?"

Probably not. I found myself doing despicable, incomprehensible things. I hung a giant Argentine flag on the living room wall of my Mexico City apartment. I began collecting Argentine memorabilia—Quilmes beer posters, maté tea gourds—that I bought at exorbitant prices from Mexican collectors. I insisted on referring to the park outside my front door by its proper name of Parque San Martin, for the Argentine independence hero, rather than Parque Mexico, which everybody in the city preferred to call it. I blew off some of the world's best restaurants—Mexico City had a sophisticated and varied palate that Buenos Aires could only dream of matching—and opted instead for a cluster of Argentine *parrillas* a few blocks from my apartment. All the steak was imported from the United States—there was an export ban on Argentine beef at the time because of an outbreak of foot-and-mouth disease—but it didn't matter to me. I cheered rabidly for Argentine soccer teams, devoured Argentine newspapers on the Internet, and fervently plotted ways to return to Buenos Aires.

It occurred to me, only after the fact, that I had done exactly as The Godfather had instructed. I had fallen in love—the honest-to-God, maddening-as-hell, till-death-do-us-part type of love—but not with a girl. I had fallen head over heels for Argentina.

HOW COULD THIS HAVE HAPPENED? IT WAS A BIT LIKE falling for an alcoholic at the very moment she hits rock bottom, sleeping in a gutter with puke in her hair. The years I spent in Argentina were arguably the worst in the country's history—and that was saying something. During my four years in Buenos Aires, I lived through an economic crash comparable in duration and scope to the Great Depression in the United States. Most of my best Argentine friends from outside the world of the milonga had left the country, probably forever. I had lost about $2,000 in an Argentine bank, my salary had been cut in half by the currency devaluation, and amid the collapse, I had inexplicably begun to go bald at the preposterous age of twenty-three.

During those long, boozy nights at the Niño Bien, I danced with far more grandmothers than twenty-year-old underwear models. I never got the girl I wanted. I couldn't master even the most moderately difficult tango steps. I spent hundreds of dollars on other men's whiskey and suffered from innumerable head-splitting hangovers. Yet, looking back, it surprises me to realize that I don't think of my memories from Argentina as being "good" or "bad." In fact, the moments of crisis and squalor turned out to be the most worthwhile. I'm back in the United States now, about to turn thirty, married, and the father of a beautiful young daughter. And what I value above all about my years in Buenos Aires is that the experiences themselves were vivid—it was the intensity that mattered most. That, more than any series of steps, is the lesson I took away from the tango.

I VISITED ARGENTINA A YEAR AFTER I LEFT AND FOUND EL Tigre svelte, wearing designer jeans, and drinking only tonic water. As was true of Argentina, his fortune had recently improved somewhat; El Tigre had played a supporting role as a corrupt cop in an Argentine movie that had enjoyed some box-office success, and he seemed less interested in the milonga than in Hollywood gossip. He was sitting by himself at Salon Canning, soberly reading the *espectáculos* section of *La Nación* in the dim light, apparently oblivious to the tangoing couples around him. I was dismayed to discover that he didn't remember me at first. Within five minutes after I sat down he asked, with a sly grin: "Have I ever told you about the time I danced with Madonna?"

"Yes," I replied. "You said she was a horrible dancer."

He blanched but quickly recovered. "Skill is irrelevant in the tango," he said. "It's all about how you carry yourself, whether you think you're the best. So Madonna was, in fact, *un fenómeno*. I never said such a thing."

I laughed. "El Tigre, I'm very happy to see you survived the crisis."

He shook his finger at me, squinting, a toothless smile spreading across his face. "You," he said. "I remember you."

"Yes?"

"Yes. The girl."

"Mariela," I said.

"Yes." He laughed. "That arrangement was beneficial for me." I stared at him.

"How much did you get?" I asked.

"Fifty pesos," he answered. "I don't remember. A standard referral. All I had to do was introduce you."

El Tigre raised his hand to call over the waiter. He saw the look on my face, then clapped his giant hand on my shoulder, grinned, and asked:

"Was it worth it?"

ACKNOWLEDGMENTS

The author would like to thank: Clive Priddle, Susan Weinberg, and everyone at PublicAffairs for taking a chance on an unconventional book, and for their patience in seeing it through; Paul Bresnick, my agent, who saw possibilities when no one else did (including myself); Sebastian Pla and Laura Lopez, without whose hospitality this book would not have been possible; Carlos Lopez, the closest thing I had in Argentina to family; Stephen Brown and Adrian Dickson, for giving me a great job at a time when I would have gladly washed windows for food; Mom and Dad, for nurturing (and then tolerating) my passion for travel; Erica and Stella, for their love even during the long hours I was hunched over my laptop; and, finally, to the people of Argentina, who I hope will see in this book a story of pure, if complicated, passion for their country.